When God Says, 'Well Done!'

To:

Mrs Kuponu

Happy Birthday!

Love
The Adegboyes
x
x.

When God Says 'Well Done!'

R. T. KENDALL

Christian Focus Publications

©1993 R. T. Kendall
ISBN 1 85792 017 1

Published in 1993 and reprinted in 2000
by
Christian Focus Publications, Geanies House,
Fearn, Ross-shire, IV20 1TW,
Scotland, Great Britain

www.christianfocus.com

Scripture quotations are from the New International Version,
published by Hodder and Stoughton.

Cover design by Donna MacLeod

Printed and bound in Great Britain by
Cox & Wyman Ltd, Reading, Berks

Contents

To
Rich and Dottie

PREFACE

My friend Robert Amess, pastor of Duke Street Baptist Church, Richmond, Surrey, cautioned me when I told him my sermon coming up on the following Sunday was on the subject of 'Reward'.

'Thinking British Christians are put off by the idea of reward', he said to me.

'I know that,' I replied, 'I haven't lived over here for nearly twenty years for nothing!'

A few years ago I slipped into the historic Church of Scotland parish church in St. Andrews. I picked up a hymnal and opened it when my eyes fell on these lines:

My God, I love Thee; not because
I hope for heaven thereby,
Nor yet because who love Thee not
Are lost eternally.

Thou, O my Jesus, Thou didst me
Upon the Cross embrace;
For me didst bear the nails and spear,
And manifold disgrace,

And griefs and torments numberless,
And sweat of agony;
Even death itself; and all for one
Who was Thine enemy.

Then why, most loving Jesus Christ,
Should I not love Thee well,
Not for the sake of winning heaven,
Or of escaping hell;

Not with the hope of gaining aught,
Not seeking a reward;
But as Thyself hast loved me,
O ever-loving Lord?

Even so I love Thee, and will love,
And in Thy praise will sing,
Solely because Thou art my God,
And my eternal King.

These majestic words, attributed to St. Francis Xavier
(1506-52), appeal to the sincere Christian's desire to love God
for what he is, not for what he can do for us. It is a desire to
which all of us may well aspire. But I have to say it is also an
attainment no biblical writer really admitted to.

I don't mean to be unfair, but I am afraid the above lines,
convincing though they are, provide a theological loophole
which the self-righteous aspect of our nature rather hastily
welcomes. The Bible was written for saints not yet glorified!

The biblical writers themselves do not envisage a maturity
this side of Heaven that is so advanced that the idea of Reward
is beneath us. On the contrary, anyone who comes to God must
'believe that he exists *and* that he rewards those who earnestly
seek him' (Heb. 11:6). 'Do not throw away your confidence;
it will be richly rewarded' (Heb. 10:35).

Such rewarding is not limited to prayer and faith; it is also
promised to us at the Judgment Seat of Christ. 'For we must
all appear before the judgment seat of Christ, that each of us

may receive what is due him for the things done while in the body, whether good or bad' (2 Cor. 5:10). I do not think many of us would question the spirituality of the Apostle Paul who said, 'I beat my body and make it my slave so that after I have preached to others, I myself will not be disqualified for the prize' (1 Cor. 9:27). The 'prize' to which Paul refers is not Heaven itself (he never questioned whether he would make it to Heaven) but what he himself calls 'reward' (1 Cor. 3:14) or 'crown' (2 Tim. 4:8); that is in *addition* to being saved.

It has become fashionable in some circles to say 'If there were no Heaven or Hell I would still be a Christian'. Not Paul, however. 'If only for this life we have hope in Christ, we are to be pitied more than all men' (I Cor. 15:19). The New Testament message was introduced by John the Baptist with the words 'Flee from the coming wrath' (Matt. 3:7). Whoever said that men and women - saved or lost - would outgrow the need to be told what awaits all people at the end of this life?

The premiss of this book is based upon the conviction that there is a Heaven and that there is a Hell. Those only who have been given saving faith, and therefore trust in Christ alone for salvation, will go to Heaven.

The preponderant theme of this book however is based upon the Apostle Paul's teaching that not all who go to Heaven will receive a Reward at the Judgment Seat of Christ. But all can. We are all without excuse.

This book will hopefully show us at least two things: (1) How to know we are going to Heaven not Hell; and (2) How we might ensure we will receive a Reward at the Judgment Seat of Christ.

As to how the idea of contempt for Reward crept into the British mentality I do not know. But I am sympathetic with it. Not only because I have lived in England for over half of my adult life but also because the thrilling parable of the vineyard

(Matt. 20:1-16) demonstrates, among other things, God's sovereign prerogative in giving the same wages to the newest Christian as the oldest. I have had to come to terms with that parable by recalling that the same writers who had the most to say about being justified before God by faith alone also had the most to say about reward (and loss of reward) to those who are justified. The parable of the vineyard was not given to refute the idea of reward, which Jesus also taught (Matt. 5:12; Matt. 10:41ff). It shows, among other things, that those who are Christians for a much shorter period can also stand side by side with the maturest saints at the Judgment Seat of Christ.

This is my second book with Christian Focus. My third with them is on the way (my treatment of Hebrews 6). What a pleasure to work with these Scots! My warmest thanks to Mr Malcolm Maclean and Mr William MacKenzie but also to Sheana Brown, this brilliant editor (whom I have never met) who has had the painful task of making my turgid prose more readable.

I take pleasure in dedicating this book to Mr and Mrs Richard Oates of Key Largo, Florida, two of our dearest friends on earth. Their love to Louise and me cannot be fully reciprocated but this dedication is a token of how we feel about them.

R. T. Kendall

London
November 1992

INTRODUCTION

On the front page of *The Times* (25 July 1992) prominence is given to a best-selling book that demonstrates the cover-up of how Marilyn Monroe died. This cover-up, it is reported, was 'so successfully stage managed that it has taken 30 years to uncover the truth'. This book implicates American politicians that were in the highest places of government. Had such been uncovered before 1963, it would have, if true, made later scandals like Watergate seem as relatively silly.

John F Kennedy is usually regarded as a twentieth century hero. Richard Nixon is now known almost entirely for being a disgraced leader. Followers of both of these men want to restore their dignity and assure their place in history as great men.

Ronald Reagan and George Bush each wants credit for ending the Cold War. You can be sure that their biographies, if not their autobiographies, will cover these areas.

The weakness of so many great men, including giants in the church, is their self-consciousness concerning their place in history; how they will be regarded by those living after they are dead. One preacher I know of even allowed a bronze statue to be made of himself - and was present for its unveiling by a famous sculptor.

Harry S Truman perhaps said it best. He refused to allow any statue to be made of himself lest future generations ask 'Who was this?'

The purpose of this book can be summed up: what people say about any of us here below does not really matter. What is said of us at the Judgment Seat of Christ does. It is *all* that really matters.

I don't know of course how much time is left before Jesus comes. I think not long. But what if Jesus tarries for another 1,000 years? And what if some are accredited with the profile of a St. Augustine, a Martin Luther or a Winston Churchill? What do you suppose will matter to them in that Day?

It may have taken 30 years to uncover the 'truth' surrounding Marilyn Monroe's death, whatever the truth really is. The wickedness that is purported to underlie her death is paralleled a thousand times over by those whose names were not known but whose hurts and humiliations were just as real. Is she the only one to have posthumous 'vindication'? What about the unknown? What of those who were walked over, misunderstood, hated, wiped out - with no trace of hope that the truth will be known?

I answer: there is coming a Day. What an ambitious journalist had to do, working through 30 years of material, to sell a book, a righteous God will do in a single day - for all underdogs. It won't be to sell a book. It won't take him 30 years.

He will do it in a Day. He will do it to clear his own Name. And everyone else's, should vindication be deserved.

> Every valley shall be raised up,
>   every mountain and hill made low;
> the rough ground shall become level,
>   the rugged places a plain.
> And the glory of the LORD will be revealed,
>   and all mankind together will see it.
>   For the mouth of the LORD has spoken' (Isa. 40:4-5).

Whatever else Isaiah the prophet meant by these words, this book comes with the promise from God that every unvindicated person will be vindicated, every 'vindicated' person (that is, when history glossed over the truth) will be uncovered. Those who were treated ruggedly will be given unspeakable bliss; those who appeared to get away with murder will suffer unspeakable agony.

Why? Because, as the psalmist put is, 'Righteousness and justice are the foundation of your throne' (Psalm 89:14). 'For God will bring every deed into judgment, including every hidden thing, whether it is good or evil (Eccl. 12:14). Jesus said to his disciples, 'There is nothing covered that will not be made known' (Matt. 10:26). 'I tell you that men will have to give account on the day of judgment for every careless word they have spoken. For by your words you will be acquitted, and by your words you will be condemned' (Matt. 12:36-37).

God can wait. So can we. He has waited for thousands of years. So must we. No-one in history has been so maligned, hated, walked over, misunderstood and unvindicated as God. Do you think God likes that? I can tell you, he does not.

One day God will clear his name. And yours - if you too have vindication coming. He won't invent things. It will come by the unveiling of the unembellished truth.

One day God will expose all frauds. Those whose 'place in history' was revered. Those whose cover-up succeeded.

If the prophet Elisha knew the very works that a wicked king spoke in his bedroom (2 Kings 6:12), what a small thing it will be for God to unveil the truth of all our words before everybody.

When we are gripped by the truth that *truth will prevail*, why do we need to speed up the process by efforts to clear our names now?

If there is anything that God loves to do most, it is to unveil the truth. God is the essence of truth. It is impossible for him to lie (Heb. 6:18). To be on good terms with him means sheer

openness before him (Psalm 51:6). Jesus is truth (John 14:6).
The Holy Spirit is the Spirit of truth (John 14:17).

What God does best - if anything he does can be measured
- is to vindicate. He is the expert. The way he does it is
unpredictable and 'beyond tracing out' (Rom. 11:33).

If there is anything God doesn't like - if his wrath against
evil can be measured - it is when one does *his* job. He doesn't
like that one bit. 'It is mine to avenge; I will repay' (Deut.
32:35).

But there is a problem. The problem is, that there is no
promise of vindication this side of the Judgment Seat of Christ.
God's word to suffering Christians is this: 'He will pay back
trouble to those who trouble you and give relief to you who are
troubled'. That sounds good to those who are hurting from
mistreatment. The trouble is that the promise is not guaranteed
during the time of our sojourn. 'This will happen when the
Lord Jesus is revealed from heaven in blazing fire with his
powerful angels' (2 Thess. 1:6-7).

What do we do in the meantime? We have only one choice,
namely, to seek the honour that comes from God only. Not the
premature, tentative and unreliable honour that comes from
man - even the best of men. But the honour that comes from
God alone. Jesus put a question to certain Jews: 'How can you
believe if you accept praise from one another, yet make no
effort to obtain the praise that comes from the only God?'
(John 5:44).

When Jesus spoke of seeking the honour that comes from
God there was an implicit promise that God wants to share his
praise for us with us - one day. Not now. 'I am the LORD; that
is my name! I will not give my glory to another' (Isa. 42:8).
But one day he will lift us up. 'Humble yourselves, therefore,
under God's mighty hand, that he may lift you up in due time'
(1 Peter 5:6).

In the meantime, we must not only lower our voices but, like Job, put our hands over our mouths (Job 40:4). This is why Paul says, 'Therefore judge nothing before the appointed time; wait till the Lord comes. He will bring to light what is hidden in darkness and will expose the motives of men's hearts. At that time each will receive his praise from God' (1 Cor. 4:5).

What about vindication now? It rarely happens. I will touch on this in Chapter 16. Once in a while God will step in and judge injustice. It is, like a miracle, a taste of the Eschaton (the Last Day) brought forward. God can do it. But I know of no biblical evidence to encourage us to expect it in advance of the Judgment. We may pray for the miraculous, yes, but to anticipate vindication prior to the Judgment Seat of Christ is to read the Bible with our eyes closed.

This book is presented to the reader with the hope that you will abandon any effort to clear your name in this life.

But there is more. This book comes to you with the prayer that you will live the *rest of your life* in the light of the Judgment Seat of Christ.

One of the reasons we have this teaching in the Bible is that the future can have an effect upon the present. In other words, the Judgment Seat of Christ is unveiled in the Bible that we might live our lives accordingly. It should make a difference now.

I guarantee one thing. If you become convinced of what I have written below it *will* make a difference in the way you live.

I wish I could guarantee that all of your eschatological questions will be answered in this book. (Eschatology means 'the doctrine of last things'.) I wish all of my own were answered! Eschatology contains some of the most mysterious and difficult problems in the whole of Christian theology.

Among these questions not answered are: (1) the meaning

of the 1,000 years in Revelation 20 or its possible connection with the time of the Second Coming; (2) the nature of our resurrected bodies; and (3) the issue of whether there is more than one Judgment - e.g. whether there is one for the unsaved and a separate one for the saved. Even if I have strong opinions on any of the above, this is not the place for treating such. I am more concerned with whether we are *ready* for the Judgment. This was Paul's preponderant concern.

A few years ago it was my privilege to stand on the remains of the ancient Bema Seat in Corinth. Archaeologists have uncovered the original site to which Paul implicitly refers when he addressed the church at Corinth:

> For we must all appear before the judgment seat of Christ,
> that each one may receive what is due him for the things done
> while in the body, whether good or bad (2 Cor. 5:10).

The translation 'judgment seat' is from the Greek word *bema*. Paul uses the same word in Romans 14:10 where he calls it 'God's judgment seat'.

The Bema Seat was well known in the ancient Graeco-Roman world. It was the tribunal, the platform on which a Roman magistrate sat, flanked by his counsellors, to administer justice. It was traditionally erected in some public place. It was the place where awards were also handed out. It could be a place of public triumph or humiliation. It was out in the open for everybody to see.

Paul simply incorporated that word and applied it to the most awesome event that will ever occur. The Old Testament prophets called it the 'day of the LORD' (Ezek. 30:3; Joel 1:15; Amos 5:18). The concept of a Final Day in which ultimate justice will be administered was so well known in ancient Judaism that Jesus only needed to refer to 'that day' in the

Sermon on the Mount (Matt. 7:22). Paul called it 'the day when God will judge man's secrets through Jesus Christ' (Rom. 2:16). Preaching at the Areopagus (called Mars Hill in the AV) Paul addressed the philosophers of Athens and informed them that God 'has set a day when he will judge the world by the man he has appointed', namely, Jesus Christ (Acts 17:31).

The writer of the Epistle to the Hebrews said, 'Man is destined to die once, and after that to face judgment' (Heb. 9:27). John had a glimpse of the Event in advance by the Holy Spirit and described it like this: 'Look, he is coming with clouds, and every eye will see him, even those who pierced him; and all the peoples of the earth will mourn because of him' (Rev 1:7).

Then I saw a great white throne and him who was seated on it. Earth and sky fled from his presence, and there was no place for them. And I saw the dead, great and small, standing before the throne, and books were opened. Another book was opened, which is the book of life. The dead were judged according to what they had done as recorded in the books. The sea gave up the dead that were in it, and death and Hades gave up the dead that were in them, and each person was judged according to what he had done. Then death and Hades were thrown into the lake of fire. The lake of fire is the second death. If anyone's name was not found written in the book of life, he was thrown into the lake of fire (Rev. 20:11-15).

Sooner or later, then, two classes of people in human history will be judged: saved and lost. The lost are those who will be punished forever in the lake of fire - Hell. They are those who will be judged without the benefit of a *covering*. They are those who, while they were alive in the present age, did not appeal to the one Mediator between God and men - the man Christ Jesus. Had they done so they would have a covering at the Final Judgment. That covering is the robe of Christ's own righteousness - given to people freely by faith in the blood of the Son of God, Jesus Christ. It is the blood of Jesus, then, that makes some exempt from the alternative punishment for sin - everlasting Hell.

The ultimate punishment for sin took place about 2,000 years ago - when Jesus Christ died on the cross. On Good Friday God punished Jesus - who never sinned - for our sins (2 Cor. 5:21). Those who appeal to Christ's blood - not their own efforts - are given an eternal pardon of their sins. They will go to Heaven, not Hell.

Hell was created for the devil and his angels (Matt. 25:41). But all those who, when standing before the Great White Throne, have no covering, will be sent to Hell.

Sin is ultimately punished two ways: either by the blood of Jesus or the fires of Hell. The fires of Hell and the blood of Jesus in a sense go together: they are the two final ways God chose to deal with sin. The fires of Hell do not truly satisfy the justice of God. This is the reason why Hell is eternal. If the fires of Hell satisfied the justice of God we could be sure that Hell would not last forever. But only the blood of Christ completely satisfies God's justice. It is like the ancient Passover: 'When I see the blood, I will pass over you' (Exod. 12:13).

I would appeal to the reader at this moment with this question: Do you know for sure that, if you were to die today, you would go to Heaven?

I asked that question of a former Prime Minister. It happened one Saturday morning on the steps of Westminster Chapel during our Pilot Light ministry. He looked at me with a bit of indignation and unbelief. 'Do you?' he asked - as if it was impossible to make such a claim!

It is not arrogance to know for sure that you will go to

Heaven. It is simply trust in Christ's infallible promise. The promise is offered to everybody. 'For God so love the world that he gave his one and only Son, that whoever believes in him shall not perish but have everlasting life' (John 3:16). It would indeed be arrogance to claim assurance of eternal life if such a gift were based upon our good works. But it is not. It is putting all our eggs into one basket: Jesus died for me.

Are you ready for the Judgment? 'Just as man is destined to die once, and after that to face judgment, so Christ was sacrificed once to take away the sins of many people; and he will appear a second time, not to bear sin, but to bring salvation to those who are waiting for him' (Heb 9:27-28). You can know that you are saved.

But there is also a judgment of the *saved*. For all I know, this judgment will come first, if I Peter 4:17-18 mirrors an eschatological order: 'For it is time for judgment to begin with the family of God; and if it begins with us, what will the outcome be for those who do not obey the gospel of God? And, "If it is hard for the righteous to be saved, what will become of the ungodly and the sinner?"'

I don't know if this aspect of the Final Judgment actually precedes the judgment of the lost. But I am sure of this: we who are saved will also be judged; not merely on the basis of whether we are saved or lost but on the basis of our lives as Christians.

It is a sobering, scary discovery for us to come to terms with the fact that the same New Testament writer who had the most to say about being justified by faith alone also had the most to say about rewards and punishments of those who have actually been justified by faith. The Apostle Paul clearly taught that we are justified (made righteous) before God by faith alone (Rom. 4:5). Faith, not works, assures us of being declared righteous before a most holy God. This assures us of going to Heaven when we die and guarantees a covering of our sins at the Judgment Seat of Christ. I shall return to this theme in this book.

But it is *no less true* that 'we [Paul includes himself] must *all* appear before the judgment seat of Christ, that each one may receive what is due to him for the deeds done while in the body, whether good or bad' (2 Cor. 5:10). I could well wish it were not true. I could wish that if I am washed by the blood of Christ I therefore need not anticipate any review of my life as a believer. That would suit me fine. But it is not true.

That is what this book is mainly about. I have chosen to deal in detail with the passages of the Apostle Paul that pertain to the Christian - not the lost - at the Judgment Seat of Christ. His teaching has been thought out by him and it is painfully clear.

This book may just come to some reader in the nick of time. I promise you, if you take seriously what follows you will be glad you did. Are you ready for the Judgment?

In October 1987 a 100 m.p.h. hurricane hit the south east of England. WHY WEREN'T WE WARNED? was the headline in one daily newspaper. Consider these words of the prophet Ezekiel:

> Son of man, I have made you a watchman for the house of Israel; so hear the word I speak and give them warning from me. When I say to a wicked man, "You will surely die," and you do not warn him or speak out to dissuade him from his evil ways in order to save his life, that wicked man will die for his sin, and I will hold you accountable for his blood. But if you do warn the wicked man and he does not turn from his wickedness or from his evil ways, he will die for his sin; but you will have saved yourself (Ezek 3:17-19).

I have no way of knowing at what stage of the Final Judgment God is going to uncover motives, lies, hurts, injustices of all men that ever lived. But I can safely promise he will do it. All those who got away with lies will be brought to court. The immoral will be openly exposed. The truth will come out. The essence of the Judgment Seat of Christ will be the revelation of the truth. Truth will prevail.

When I was a boy growing up in Ashland, Kentucky, we used to sing this song. In those days the singing of this hymn was often accompanied by conviction of sin, especially if it followed a sermon on the Judgment Seat of Christ:

There's a great day coming, a great day coming;
There's a great day coming by and by,
When the saints and the sinners shall be parted right and left.
Are you ready for that day to come?

There's a bright day coming, a bright day coming;
There's a bright day coming by and by,
But its brightness shall only come to them that love the Lord.
Are you ready for that day to come?

There's a sad day coming, a sad day coming;
There's a sad day coming by and by.
When the sinner shall hear his doom, 'Depart, I know ye not!'
Are you ready for that day to come?

Chorus
Are you ready for that day to come?
Are you ready? Are you ready?
Are you ready for the judgment day?
Are you ready for the judgment day?

That hymn of course was directed mainly to the person who had not yet embraced Jesus Christ as Lord and Saviour.

But it is none the less a fair question to ask any believer who reads these lines: Are *you* ready for the Judgment?

1

Low Profile, High Pay

> I planted the seed, Apollos watered it, but God made it grow.
> So neither he who plants nor he who waters is anything, but
> only God, who makes things grow. The man who plants and
> the man who waters have one purpose, and each will be
> rewarded according to his own labour (1 Corinthians 3:6-8).

Paul is addressing those believers that he calls 'carnal' or
'worldly'. They have been guilty of hero-worship, and in the
meantime, they have forfeited 'meat'. In fact, he puts it to them
like this in the preceding verses:

> I gave you milk, not solid food, for you were not yet ready for
> it. Indeed, you are still not ready. You are still worldly. For
> since there is jealousy and quarrelling among you, are you not
> worldly? Are you not acting like mere men? For when one
> says, "I follow Paul," and another, "I follow Apollos," are
> you not mere men? (1 Corinthians 3:2-4)

Paul's intention is to wean the Corinthians from 'milk', that
they might eventually take 'meat' for he wants each of them to
receive a reward at the judgment seat of Christ. Meat is a word
Paul uses to refer to *spiritual* (not necessarily theological)
maturity. It means the ability to hear God's voice. Some assume
that by 'meat' Paul refers to deeper theological truths like
predestination. A lot of Christians grasp predestination but have

cold hearts and therefore cannot hear the Holy Spirit's voice.

That is why the Hebrew Christians were rebuked for being 'dull of hearing' (Heb. 5:11, AV). Having warned of the danger of repeating history – the children of Israel in the wilderness who did not hear the Holy Spirit (Heb. 3:7-11) – the writer fears that these Hebrew Christians would reach the place where they would be stone deaf! When one reaches that sad state it is impossible for him or her to be renewed again to repentance (Heb. 6:4-6). Meat, then refers to the inner spiritual sensitivity to hear the Holy Spirit speaking.

Paul's method is twofold: first, to show who it is that does the saving, and what the role is of each person involved in conversion, lest we admire any one person too much. After all, it is God who makes things happen. Second: that we are all going to stand before the judgment seat of Christ and we, not the person who led us to the Lord, will give an account of our own life.

God's mathematics

There are two operative words in this text: the first is the word 'one'; the second is the word 'own'. 'The man who plants and the man who waters have *one* purpose, and each will be rewarded according to his *own* labour.' So the two roles of planting and watering, when added up are one. It is what *God* does, no matter how many plant and how many water. God makes things grow. One plus one equals one - that is God's mathematics! Ten plus ten equals one; one hundred plus one hundred equals one: God, who makes things grow.

When all is said and done, all Christian ministry boils down to two things - salvation and sanctification. What we do will be aimed either towards those outside the church, or directed to those who are within the church. But according to Paul, added up they become one:

From him the whole body, joined and held together by every
supporting ligament, grows and builds itself up in love, as
each part does its work (Ephesians 4:16).

I intend to examine 1 Corinthians 3:8 in considerable detail
as there are a number of points I want to explore.

The first is *teamwork*. The Oxford English Dictionary defines
team as 'a set of people working together'. Why? They are one.
This will mean that *each member surrenders a high profile*.
For those who have an ego problem this is quite a task! You
say, Well, this won't apply to me, I don't have a problem with
ego. Don't you? Let me ask you a question: if you look at a
group photograph you are in, whose face do you look for first?

The bruised ego
The winning team is one where each puts winning ahead of
personal profile. When one member is more determined to get
recognition in the team, the result is losing. What is it that
causes disunity in the church every time? It is the bruised,
vindictive ego. In order for a team to be a team, there must be
the willingness for each to have a low profile.

So the operative word, *one*, leads to another word, *surrender* - of seven things. First, surrender of identity; second,
surrender of independence; third, surrender of individuality;
fourth, surrender of inflexibility; fifth, surrender of indiffer-
ence; sixth, surrender of inequality and seventh, surrender of
personal interest. Incidentally, it is not a question whether or
not we will result in one, because God will see to that. What
is sobering is how this oneness will happen. Either we will do
it voluntarily, and get a reward - that means high pay, or we do
it involuntarily and suffer loss - which means no reward.

The second point in this verse is *talent*. The man who plants
- is that your talent? The man who waters - is that your talent?

Planting and watering are metaphors that refer to the kind of ministry that God gives to particular Christians. Now that does not mean that they have to be one or the other for Paul was both. The point is that each Christian has a gift and all of these combined together add up to one.

A small fish in a big pond

The third point is *test*. What is that? It is the willingness to become one. This happens when all you have done has gone unnoticed and you do not get recognition. If Paul had said, 'I have planted and God gave the increase,' there would be room for self-importance. How humbling it is that God uses more than one person in another's conversion! There is not a single one of us who owes his or her conversion and growth just to one person. In my case I could speak not of a dozen but of fifty, maybe a hundred, all of whom have had a powerful influence on me. The test is the willingness to be a small fish in a big pond.

What if I am not noticed for all the hard work I do? My effectiveness must be determined by (a) my willingness to be insignificant and have an insignificant part, and (b) my willingness to have an unnoticed part. Great men show themselves small when they become too worried about their place in history. Politicians and historians argue as to who is most responsible for the Cold War.

But what does it matter? In a short time we will all stand before the judgment seat of Christ, where it will all come out. People who are so eager to have their biographies say this or that about themselves will find out that one day we will *all* know the real truth anyway! The question is, If I am a peacemaker, will I keep quiet about it? If I am persecuted, will I keep quiet about it? If I am pious, if I pray, fast and give sacrificially, will I keep quiet about it? If I am determined to get noticed, well, I will probably get it, but that means I get paid *now*, but recognition in this life is very low pay indeed.

As we move on to Paul's second operative word, *own*, we come to the fourth point in this verse: *totality*. Notice how it is put: 'every man', each person. What does this mean - *each person*? It means that, although *all* we do in this life is mixed in God's melting pot, so that our efforts become one, our individual contributions are not really lost after all. The totality of the body of Christ will stand before the judgment seat of Christ and yet every one of us will be assessed. Not a single person and their actions will escape being noticed. The knowledge of standing before the judgment seat of Christ had such an effect on Paul that he wrote, 'Since ... we know what it is to fear the Lord, we try to persuade men' (2 Corinthians 5:11). I love the Authorised Version here: 'knowing the terror of the Lord, we persuade men'.

Believing this makes a difference now
If you really do believe *you* are going to stand before the judgment seat of Christ it will affect your conduct here below. I refer to Paul again, this time in Romans 14:10:

> You, then, why do you judge your brother? Or why do you look down on your brother? For we will all stand before God's judgment seat.

Someone once asked me, What do you think of so-and-so and what he has done? I replied that my opinion does not matter since it will not be long before everybody will know the truth as we stand before the judgment seat of Christ. I may want to judge you, but if I knew that in ten minutes I was going to stand before God, I would keep my mouth shut.

Grace to keep quiet

Not just apostles, not just ministers, not just deacons but the totality of the body of Christ shall be judged: every person shall receive their own reward according to their own labour. Every man, every woman, every function, every gift, every talent, all we ever did will be projected on God's gigantic screen. Even that time you got hurt and kept quiet about it. Those years you paid your tithes and it hurt, but you kept quiet about it; those moments when you dignified the trial but kept quiet about it; that person you totally forgave but you kept quiet about it; or the one you stayed up with all night and helped, but kept quiet about it. Each will be rewarded according to his own labour.

The fifth point in the text is *time*. When will all this happen? And what does *each will be rewarded* mean? This refers to the future, and perhaps this disappoints you. We all want to be paid now! Yet every man *will* receive. If we have high profile now we can only expect low pay then; if we have low profile now we can look for high pay then! We may wish it had said, 'Every man *receives* his own reward' in the present tense. That way I am guaranteed recognition now; that way I'm guaranteed dividends now. But must we get our pay today?

Do you only get involved in a particular activity of the church if you think it is working? Do you do something because immediately you get results? God can, and often does, bless obedience now, but our motive may betray that we cannot wait for the judgment seat of Christ. How much better that you continually remember that you will yet stand before God and give an account of the things you did throughout life. It will be worth it all to hear two words from Jesus, 'Well done'.

The sixth point in this verse is *treasure*. Notice every man will receive his own *reward*. Now where that operative word *one* means 'surrender', the operative word *own* means 'discovery'. What I did in life that was swallowed up and unnoticed will be found out and blazed in headlines and discovered *then*. Paul's word, translated 'reward', is the Greek word, *misthon*, used twenty-nine times in the New Testament. On two or three occasions it is translated 'wages', and I have read one scholar who is convinced that Paul means that everyone will receive his own wages. I would not want to push that too far.

The reward is not heaven

The Bible often talks about reward. Nevertheless it is not just heaven we are referring to. Yet some people regard heaven as the reward. All who are saved *are* going to go to heaven but not all who go to heaven will receive a reward. This may be new theology to you, but you need to understand that. You may have thought, 'Well, if I am saved, I am saved, and I am not going to worry about anything else.' When you stand before the judgment seat of Christ even though you are not going to go to hell, you will see then why Paul stressed it again and again. Listen to the words of Jesus in the Sermon on the Mount:

> Blessed are you when people insult you, persecute you and falsely say all kinds of evil against you because of me. Rejoice and be glad, because great is your *reward* in heaven (Matthew 5:11,12).

> Be careful not to do your 'acts of righteousness' before men, to be seen by them. If you do, you will have no *reward* from your Father in heaven (Matthew 6:1).

> Do not store up for yourselves treasures on earth, where moth and rust destroy, and where thieves break in and steal. But store up for yourselves *treasures* in heaven, where moth and rust do not destroy, and where thieves do not break in and steal. For where your treasure is, there your heart will be also (Matthew 6:19-21).

When workers get their pay-packet they decide whether to spend it all now or put some in the bank. So when you are tempted to take recognition, you can put it on deposit or you can just spend it. There is a chance to get your spiritual recognition-pay now, for instance, by getting even with that person by snapping back, by reminding people that what they did was wrong. Although you are right, and you 'win', and receive your pay, that is it. You drew out what could have been on deposit in heaven. Only it is low pay. You really lost.

What is the high pay? I do not really know. Paul uses three words, as far as I know to describe it: reward, praise, crown. Peter also uses the expression: 'you will receive a rich welcome' into the kingdom when you die (2 Peter 1:11). But this assumes a certain conduct (2 Peter 1:5-8). Not all will receive this welcome.

What is the high pay? What is the reward? What is the crown? As I have said I do not know for sure what that is, but I am sure it is worth waiting for. And I am sure I am not alone. Many of you will want to hear from the lips of Jesus himself: 'Well done'. I call that high pay!

The seventh point is *trial*. Consider how Paul puts it. He says, 'The man who plants and the man who waters have one purpose, and each will be rewarded according to his own labour'. God does not forget: he keeps perfect records. But, thank God, here is the good news, he does not keep a record of wrongs confessed.

> If we confess our sins, he is faithful and just to forgive us our sins and to purify us from all unrighteousness (1 John 1:9).

What will not be known then

It is also worth remembering that God will not throw up our sins at us at the judgment seat of Christ, when we have repented of them. When Joseph forgave his brothers, he made the interpreter leave the room so that nobody in Egypt would know that they had betrayed Joseph (Genesis 45:1). The proof of total forgiveness is you do not want people to know what so-and-so did to you. As long as you want to let the cat out of the bag, as long as you want your hurt to be known, you have not forgiven. But God's forgiveness is greater: as far as the east is from the west so far are our transgressions removed from us. Sin confessed and repented of is sin that God will not bring up.

But I do believe two things will show up and be out in the open at the judgment seat of Christ. One is unconfessed sin and the other is quiet obedience.

Now why do I use the word *trial*? I do so because in verse 13 of this chapter, Paul wrote, '... his work will be shown up for what it is, because the day will bring it to light. It will be revealed with fire, and the fire will *test* the quality of each man's work.' That is a trial. We will be dealing with this in the subsequent chapters.

2

The Mystery of God's Sovereignty

For we are God's fellow workers; you are God's
field, God's building (1 Corinthians 3:9).

Behind the reward the Christian will receive at the judgment
seat of Christ lies the apostle Paul's teaching on the mystery
of God's sovereignty. We are being prepared for that Day of
days. If we lose a reward we can only blame ourselves. But if
we receive a reward it is owing to God's grace. It is a mystery!
Before we look at the foundation and superstructure we must
see how Paul's mind works in anticipation of these. We will
therefore examine 1 Corinthians 3:9.

This text is in two parts: you will notice the distinction
between 'we' and 'you'. 'We' are labourers together with
God, 'you' are God's field, 'you' are God's building. The 'we'
refers to verses 5-8:

What, after all, is Apollos? And what is Paul? Only servants,
through whom you came to believe - as the Lord assigned to
each his task. I planted the seed, Apollos watered it, but God
made it grow. So neither he who plants nor he who waters is
anything, but only God, who makes this grow. The man who
plants and the man who waters have one purpose ...

Paul summarises his previous remarks by saying, 'we are

God's fellow workers' referring to those in ministry. But his description of the Corinthian Christians as the field, or the building, shows the response to ministry – his readers' part. What lies behind these metaphors? I can only call it the 'mystery' of God's sovereignty.

The sovereignty of God

If you are a new Christian then perhaps you have overheard this phrase, the sovereignty of God. The sovereignty of God refers to God's will and ability *without* our input. God has a will of his own; he decides things without our counsel and without our help. God is able to do what he decides, and can even carry it out without our assistance. It is as though he stands alone apart from us. 'Our God is in heaven; he does whatever pleases him' (Psalm 115:3). What is so mysterious about that? Is it not that straightforward? But it *is* a mystery, for Paul says, 'We are God's fellow workers'. For reasons known to God alone he has decided to bring *us* into the picture!

The mystery is that he *chose* to use us and turns things over to us as *though* it is entirely left to us although he remains independent and sovereign. The fact is that God chose to use humans in the work of ministry for he *could* have saved people directly, without involving us at all. All of us, however, are converted because somebody witnessed to us; somebody brought us to church; somebody handed us a tract or we heard preaching. God did not stop you right in your tracks without the gospel and reveal himself to you immediately by the power of the Holy Spirit. He could have given you a vision. But God's method is stated by Paul in 1 Corinthians 1:21:

> For since in the wisdom of God the world through its wisdom did not know him, God was pleased through the foolishness of what was preached to save those who believe.

A very difficult subject

Because we are fellow workers with God, two questions emerge, rather automatically and naturally: first, what is it that we do? and second, what is it that God does? We are dealing with possibly the most difficult subject in Christian theology. And if you think I am going to resolve it, you are going to be disappointed, for it is a mystery. The word, mystery, means a matter that is hidden. Certain data is kept from us; we do not know it all. We do not understand everything.

I think the best illustration of this point is the story of Moses at the foot of Mount Sinai. He had been there many times before, but one day he noticed what appeared to be a brush fire, a bush on fire. He began to notice the bush was not consumed although the fire continued to burn. Moses thought he had better go see what it was. And he got so far before God said, 'Do not come any closer. Take off your sandals, for the place where you are standing is holy ground' (Exodus 3:5).

So when it comes to the sovereignty of God we must straight away call it a mystery. We might want to get up close and see how could all this be. God says, 'Stop. Don't come any closer. It's holy ground.' Paul understood this better than anybody. This is what he said:

> Oh, the depth of the riches of the wisdom and knowledge of God! How unsearchable his judgments, and his paths beyond tracing out! Who has known the mind of the Lord? Or who has been his counsellor? (Romans 11:33).

Two Levels

To help us deal with the mystery of God's sovereignty, we need to see it at two levels. The first level is that of Christian ministry, that is, trying to reach the lost. The second level is that of Christian discipleship: our response to the gospel and subsequently to Christian teaching. To express it differently the first level refers to us being fellow workers with God while on the second level we are God's field, we are his building.

Christian ministry

At this first level, we can briefly answer our two original questions: what is it we do? what is it God does? Fundamentally, what we do who preach, teach, or are involved in pastoral care is roughly something like this: we answer the call; we prepare ourselves for service; we get knowledge, sometimes training; we walk in the light; we remain available; we go when he says go.

A short summary of what *God* does can also be simply stated. First, he tells us what to say - we are not given a choice about that. Second, he equips us. Third, he opens doors. Fourth, he sends people to us that he has chosen to save. Fifth, he works at both ends when we are obedient, so that if I am faithful in preaching, God will help me to speak, and he will work at the other end, dealing with the hearts of those who hear what I say. Spontaneous combustion then takes place: the work of the Spirit cannot be stopped and the person hearing me becomes a believer. That therefore is something God does. It is known as *effectual calling*.

C. H. Spurgeon was converted in a Methodist church. One day he was sitting in church, listening to a rather boring sermon. He later said, 'The thought struck me, How did I become a Christian? I sought the Lord. Well how did I come to seek the Lord? The truth flashed across my mind in a moment: I should not have sought him unless there had been some previous influence in my mind to make me seek him. But I prayed, thought I, and then I asked myself, How came I to pray? Well, I was induced to pray by reading the scriptures. How came I to read the scriptures? I did read them, but what led me to do so. Then, in a moment, I saw God was at the bottom of it all and that he was the author of my faith, and so the whole doctrine of grace opened up to me and from that doctrine I have not departed to this day and I desire to make this my constant confession, I ascribe my change wholly to the Lord.'

I call Paul's description that 'we are fellow workers with God' the most beautiful combination that ever was! A denial of that combination is either to say we do it all, which means that there is no such thing as the sovereignty of God and work of the Holy Spirit, or on the other extreme, God does it all without us which shows contempt for the great commission to go into all the world and to preach the gospel to every creature. To accept the combination, that we are God's fellow workers, is to admit to a mystery. There is a word which describes this mystery: it is the word *antinomy*. It means two parallel principles that are irreconcilable but *both* true! Jim Packer, in his classic book, *Evangelism and the Sovereignty of God*, said that an antinomy, theologically, should be defined as two irreconcilable principles that are *apparently* irreconcilable, but are both true.

I remember, as a little boy, that on the way to school we could walk right down a rail-road track for about a mile. I remember once how I stood in the middle of the track with the rail on both sides parallel to me, but the further away they got, it looked like they came together. Spurgeon himself said, that when you come to the sovereignty of God and human responsibility, they are parallel, but they do not meet in this life, they meet in eternity.

There is an apocryphal story, but I have always thought there was something sweet about it. Jesus returned to heaven after finishing his work on earth. He sat down at the right hand of God and the angels welcomed him.

They said to him, 'Is your work finished?'

He said, 'It is finished.'

'What happens now?'

'Well, I have given my word to my disciples, those whom God gave me.'

'What happens then?'

'They will give the word to others.'

'And what happens after that?'

'I have no other plan.'

Christian discipleship

When Paul says: 'You are God's field, God's building', he is elaborating on the second part of verse 8. He mixes the metaphors - field and building. The field refers to *natural* growth of plants, vegetation and trees. That implication can be seen when Paul says, 'I planted the seed, Apollos watered it, but God made it grow'. The building, however, refers to a *superstructure* above the foundation. So there are two metaphors. He began with the metaphor of natural growth and we might have expected him to continue with that one, but he stopped. Suddenly he changed metaphors and introduced 'building' and he never returns to the idea of the field. From then on it was 'building' and all that he goes on to say about the judgment seat of Christ, has to do with the building.

You will see this in verse 10: 'By the grace God has given me, I laid a foundation as an expert builder'; and in verse 11: 'For no-one can lay any foundation other than the one already laid, which is Jesus Christ. If any man builds on this foundation using gold, silver, costly stones ...' So that once he brought in building he stays with that; he does not return to the idea of planting, of vegetation, of fruit. Incidentally, there is a third metaphor in 1 Corinthians 3, down in verse 16 where he says, 'Don't you know that you yourselves are God's *temple* and that God's Spirit lives in you? If anyone destroys God's temple, God will destroy him; for God's temple is sacred, and you are that temple.'

In subsequent chapters, we will return to the question of building, but in this chapter I want to concentrate on the mystery of God's sovereignty with reference to 'field'. 'You are God's field.' It is what we all are, a reference to all of us who are saved, including those in the ministry. That means all of us.

There are two parallel passages in the New Testament that I know of, there may be others, that show how Paul might have developed more fully the metaphor of 'field'. The first is in John 15, when Jesus said, 'I am the true vine and my Father is the gardener.' The second is Hebrews 6:7-8:

> Land that drinks in the rain often falling on it and that produces a crop useful to those for whom it is farmed receives the blessing of God. But land that produces thorns and thistles is worthless and is in danger of being cursed. In the end it will be burned.

Fire

Within these metaphors it is interesting to note the common reference to *fire*. You find it in the metaphor of the building in 1 Corinthians 3 where Paul talks about the hay and straw being burned up and believers being saved by fire. Jesus, in John 15:6, says: 'If anyone does not remain in me, he is like a branch that is thrown away and withers; such branches are picked up, thrown into the fire and burned.' Again in Hebrews 6:8 we read: 'In the end it will be burned'. The reference to fire in all of these passages is not accidental.

As we look at the sovereignty of God and believers I will stress two aspects: *ownership* and *obligation*.

We cannot really run from God

It is intrinsic to understanding God's sovereignty that we realise what Paul meant when he said that Christians are God's field. He is showing that God owns us. This simply means that God has total rights to our lives. We have no private life; our private life is his. We cannot go on a two-week holiday and say, 'God, I want a good time and you have been breathing down my neck for most of the year. I would like a couple of weeks away from you.' No, he'll go *with* us on holiday; we have no time that we can call our own. It is his time. We have no secret thoughts about which we can say, 'God, I just don't want you to know about'. We do not own ourselves.

Does this disturb and annoy you? Or does this thrill you to your finger-tips to know that you are bought with a price? It is true whether you like it or not! You are his; he owns you. You are God's field, it is not your field. For that reason God can do what he wants with you, and because you are his, you cannot even get rid of him if you tried. You may have said to God, 'Leave me alone'. But he didn't, he would not.

Because he owns us God has an obligation. God ultimately takes the responsibility, not only for saving us, but also for our development.

> Every virtue we possess and every conquest won
> And every thought of holiness are his alone.
>
> (Harriet Auber)

It is a mystery that God, who chose me in Christ before the foundation of the world, works for my growth.

I am the true vine and my Father is the gardener. He cuts off every branch in me that bears no fruit, while every branch that does bear fruit he prunes so that it will be even more fruitful (John 15:1-2).

How God makes things happen

To ensure this growth God has something ready to make it happen: *chastening*. Chastening is *enforced learning*. 'For whom the Lord loves, he chastens and scourges every son whom he receives' (AV). Or as the NIV puts it, '... the Lord disciplines those he loves, and he punishes everyone he accepts as a son' (Hebrews 12:6). To 'scourge' literally means to whip with thongs and God can be rugged in his dealings with us. Why does he institute chastening? That we share in his holiness (Hebrews 12:10).

There are three stages of chastening, in this order: *internal*, *external*, and although we hope it does not happen there is stage three, *terminal* chastening.

Internal chastening is when God just deals with you by the word, the Bible. It is happening perhaps right now. I just trust that you are feeling the cutting word of God, that sword with two edges, piercing you. Thank God for that. It is internal chastening and it is the best way to have your problem solved.

But if that does not work there is stage two, external chastening. The external chastening is providence, as illustrated in the life of Jonah. Jonah was told, 'Go to Nineveh'. When he disobeyed, God arranged for Jonah to be swallowed by a fish. Ultimately, Jonah prayed to God.

If chastening by the external means of providence does not work, there is stage three: terminal chastening. It is very sad. I do not say how often it happens, but Jesus said, 'He cuts off every branch in me that bears no fruit' (John 15:2). I will examine this form of chastening in a later chapter.

How we make things happen

It is necessary to remember that as God's field, the true vine, we have the responsibility to be obedient. For if there is no obedience there will be no fruit to grow on that field. We are told in John 15:8 what the gardener wants: 'This is to my Father's glory, that you bear much fruit'. What is required is abiding or remaining in Christ:

> Remain in me, and I will remain in you. No branch can bear fruit by itself; it must remain in the vine. Neither can you bear fruit unless you remain in me (John 15:4).

We cannot do things our way and still abide or remain in him. Abiding in him means obedience. So you can see why the mystery of God's sovereignty is not limited to his saving work. He alone *makes things happen* in the work of sanctification, but *without my obedience* there will be no sanctification. It is, as I say, a mystery.

The second aspect of the believer's responsibility is *observation* of what we are within ourselves. The crops in a field are observable, are they not? What is required therefore is that I examine myself. Is there fruit? This refers mainly to the fruit of the Spirit, which is love, joy, peace, patience, kindness, goodness, faithfulness, gentleness and self-control. Some would push it to mean seeing other people saved and if you do not produce fruit, that is, conversions, then you are not bearing fruit. However I do not believe that is what it means.

Objectivity about ourselves

We have to observe ourselves or as Paul says, 'A man ought to examine himself.' If I examine myself it means I must have objectivity about myself. It is as though I stand back and look at myself; I observe myself. And if I see something that is not right, I deal with it. Paul calls this 'judging' ourselves. He says, 'But if we judged ourselves, we would not come under judgment.' If by the word of God or by external chastening, I judge myself, I will not have further chastening. Yet Paul does say that when we are judged, it is chastening: 'When we are judged by the Lord, we are being disciplined so that we will not be condemned with the world' (1 Corinthians 11:28-32). So that even the terminal chastening, when we are taken away and saved by fire, shows that we were saved. We suffer loss but will be saved, so as by fire. Even when God steps in like that, it proves the person was a Christian.

I have long had the conviction that the teaching of the judgment seat of Christ is one of God's internal means of producing holiness. Martin Luther once said, 'When I get to heaven I expect to be surprised three times. First, there will be those there that I didn't expect to be there. There will be some missing that I thought would be there. But the greatest surprise will be that I am there myself.' But I sometimes paraphrase that. I suspect I will have three surprises. The first is, there will be those that I expected to get a reward but who will be saved by fire. There will be those who got a reward that I thought would be saved by fire. But the greatest surprise of all is, if by the grace of God I will not be saved by fire, and find that there was something that lingered on, gold, silver, precious stones.

We will examine what it means to be saved by fire in a later chapter.

3

Following God's Blueprint

> By the grace God has given me, I laid a foundation as an
> expert builder, and someone else is building on it. But each
> one should be careful how he builds (1 Corinthians 3:10).

When Paul says he has laid the foundations this implies an
architectural plan, for one can only lay a foundation intelligently if there is a plan or a blueprint. If Paul laid the
foundation by the grace of God, then it follows we can only
intelligently build upon that foundation if we recognise that we
do it in the persevering grace of God.

An architectural plan
A blueprint is a blue photographic print of building plans: a
detailed scheme, or plan. So when Paul says, 'By the grace
God has given me, I laid a foundation as an expert builder'
behind all this there are at least three assumptions. The first is
that God has drawn up an architectural plan for the church, and
that plan includes a foundation and superstructure.

The second assumption is that Paul himself has had a look
at God's blueprint. He would not lay a foundation without
seeing a blueprint. When did he see it? We need only look at
Galatians 1:11,12 where Paul says:

> I want you to know, brothers, that the gospel I preached is not
> something that man made up. I did not receive it from any man, nor
> was I taught it; rather, I received it by revelation from Jesus Christ.

In Galatians 1:17, he says:

> ... nor did I go up to Jerusalem to see those who were apostles before I was, but I went immediately into Arabia and later returned to Damascus.

It was during this time that Paul had a look at God's blueprint.

The third assumption is that he followed that blueprint, when he says, 'I laid a foundation'. In laying the foundation he did not try to improve upon God's own scheme; he did not argue with the architect, as some builders are prone to do. Notice how he says it, 'By the grace God has given me, I laid a foundation as an expert builder'. What is the sign of the expert? It is to follow God's blueprint. Remember this: God has a blueprint for the church; he has a blueprint for you and me.

An acknowledged possession

There is a second thing we see in this text: it is an acknowledged possession. Notice how he puts it: 'By the grace God has given me'. Normally in the New Testament, references to the grace of God would have to do with being saved, for example Ephesians 2:8-9: 'For it is by grace you have been saved, through faith - and this not from yourselves, it is the gift of God - not by works, so that no-one can boast.' But here Paul particularises grace and it means two things: (1) vocation and (2) the ability to fulfil that vocation. Paul recognised that his own vocation was to be an apostle, but when he says 'by the grace God has given me' he is also showing how God gave him the ability to fulfil that vocation. When God calls you to do something, he will give you the grace to do it. All believers have a two-fold responsibility.

Playing our part

First, they have been *called to holiness*. 'It is God's will that you should be sanctified: that you should avoid sexual immorality' (1 Thessalonians 4:3). For God did not call us to be impure, but to live a holy life (1 Thessalonians 4:7). Secondly, we are not only called to holiness, but also *to find our niche in the church, and in life*. We are to know what God wants us to do in the church and in our lives. Perhaps you are more anxious to know what it is you are to do in life, and then you say, 'I'll do what I am supposed to do in the church'. But that is to reverse the order God has in mind. The call to holiness is a call to do his will and God has his heart set upon the church. It is not likely you will know what to do with your life, until you have found your niche in the church. This is a good reason for becoming a member of the church. It is so easy just to stay on the sidelines and say, 'One of these days I am going to get involved' and the years go by, wasted years. You suffer and the church suffers. It is imperative that you discover what God wants you to do and go ahead with it in the church and in your life.

Paul acknowledged the grace given to him. Now I do not question that it was partly an inherent, natural gift. Dr Clyde Narramore says, 'Your natural gift is God's hint what to do with your life'. God had his hand on the apostle Paul before he was saved and the same is true of us. Our being saved was no accident. God had his eye on us before we were converted, before we even were conscious of God, before we were aware of any restlessness of our life which we did not see at the time was the Holy Spirit getting us ready. God had his eye on us from before we were born, even from the foundation of the world. But just as Paul never knew his real potential until he was converted, neither can any of us discover our niche in life until we walk in the light.

Part of our responsibility in acknowledging the grace given

to us, which is our possession, is to come face to face with what
our abilities are. Now this can be very painful for some of us,
not just with recognising our limitations, but also realising
what we can do. We must live within the limit of our gift, but
also up to the level of responsibility that our gift requires. Do
not covet another person's gift but admit what you know is
your own gift and responsibility.

How to discover your gift
The logical step forward is to explore ways in which our gifts
can be recognised. Let me pose three questions to help in this
discovery.

The first is: *What do you enjoy?* What your gift is, is often
what you like to do. And you say, 'Well, I couldn't have
imagined that to be something *God* would want me to do.' I
never will forget, back in 1954, when God used a Scotsman,
Dr John Logan, who was ministering in America, to make me
come to terms with the fact that God had called me to preach.
I went back to Ashland, Kentucky, and revealed to my pastor
that I felt called to preach, and his comment was, 'I have been
waiting for you to see this; I'm not surprised.' I asked, 'Why
do you say that?' He replied, 'Well, for one thing, R T, all you
ever do is talk about the Bible.' I said, 'Well, doesn't everybody?' He said, 'No.' That made me see something that I
hadn't really recognised before - that others were different,
they may love the Bible and read it and be serving the Lord,
but I just lived in it. And that was one of the reasons, I think,
I had postponed recognising a call to preach, because I almost
felt guilty if I thought I had to do that, because that was what
I loved more than anything.

The second question is: *What do you feel is right for you?*
I often quote Romans 14:19: 'Do what leads to peace'. That
does refer to church unity of course and one does what makes

for peace when there is a tension here or there, but I think equally it refers to *internal* peace. You do what will give you peace inside. 'To thine own self be true' as Shakespeare said. Take a person who operates at the level of his incompetence: he is tired all the time. This is what causes nervous break-downs. A person is exhausted, overtired because they are living at a level where they are just not able to function. And sometimes their pride will not let them admit to themselves, 'I can't do this.' When this happens you need to step back, admit that it is not your gift, and do what leads to peace. On the other hand, if you live *beneath* the level of your competence and you operate beneath what you can do you will also be frustrated. You need to ask yourself, what is right for me?

The third question, *What do others recognise in you?* If God has called you to preach there will be open doors, people will want you.

And so, whatever your gift, if your gift is talking to people and counselling, they will seek you out. And there will be those who say that this is what you are good at, and sometimes we do not like it. We do not like to be told what are not good at or what we are good at. But we need to hear it and come to terms with it.

An accomplished performance

At this point Paul looks back favourably at what has been achieved: an accomplished performance. 'By the grace God has given me, I laid a foundation as an expert builder'. Paul can refer now to two accomplished facts. Twice the aorist tense is used. First, he says, 'grace was given to me'. Second, that 'I have laid the foundation.' No regrets. He had done this four years before. He says, 'I have laid it'. He had no apologies; he felt good. He had been true to the blueprint. It is equally wonderful to know that you have done God's will, and to know that you are doing God's will.

An authorised procedure

Paul did not do everything. He laid the foundation, but another built on it. There comes a time when you try to help another person, and you do your best, and you counsel, you talk, and you give the best advice - but in the end it is up to them.

Now we have an important question to ask, and how we interpret this verse from this point, shapes the way we look at the following verses in 1 Corinthians 3 and I possibly researched this more than anything else in this chapter. What does he mean when he says, 'I laid a foundation ... and someone else is building on it'? Is he now talking about Apollos? The answer is, No. This is why Paul changed the metaphor, from watering to building. When he was speaking of vegetation he said, 'I planted, Apollos watered', but he changed the metaphor because the section that follows is not addressed with Apollos in mind.

The section that follows is not addressed to the one who waters, it is not addressed to the one who teaches or who ministers because the superstructure is not in the hands of teachers or preachers. The superstructure is in the hands of believers and God has authorised them to erect the superstructure. I have read one commentary after another and I have noticed that those who look at the whole chapter, superficially, say he is talking about teachers. They are wrong. Those who have looked at it in detail have seen that Paul has very carefully brought the metaphor to a point and then changes it in order to put the responsibility upon the believers at Corinth. Leon Morris comments, 'Some restrict the application of this passage to the work of teachers. While it is especially true of teachers, it is also true in a measure of every believer that is engaged in building on the foundation.'

The awesome privilege

We come to the last point that I want to make from this verse: the awesome privilege. Week by week in my preaching ministry I may lay a foundation but my hearers build the superstructure; that is up to them. That is why we read, 'But each one should be careful how he builds'. I can tell them what God's Word says, and I can show them the blueprint, but I cannot control how they live their lives from week to week. I do not know what goes on in the secret recesses of their hearts. Let everyone be *careful* how he builds.

And so as the author I have in a sense laid the foundation and that foundation is theological, following God's blueprint. The question is where do we go from here? The superstructure is up to you. I have a superstructure to build concerning my own personal life and I must decide whether I am going to walk in the light God gives me or not. I must decide whether or not I believe what I preach and walk in my own light, if I may put it that way.

I may have a severer judgment. In fact, James 3:1 says: 'we who teach will be judged more strictly'. So, at the judgment seat of Christ, I am going to have a tougher time than many of you! I will be judged more severely. It is a scary thing! But ultimately, you will have to stand by yourself. I can live with what I preach or write, but what you do with it, is up to you. And your reward, or lack of it, will be based upon your own superstructure; your own reward or lack of it, will be based upon how well you fulfilled the grace given to you.

4

The Unchangeable Foundation

For no-one can lay any foundation other than the one
already laid, which is Jesus Christ (1 Corinthians 3:11).

What we are told in this verse is that when Paul laid the
foundation in Corinth some four years earlier, he was doing
nothing more than following God's architectural blueprint.

Although verse 11 literally reads in the Greek, 'Nobody is
able to lay another foundation,' that does not mean that some
would not *try* to lay another. What it means is that one cannot
do it with any kind of divine approval, or permission. In New
Testament times, two groups in particular were guilty of this.
The first group were the Gnostics who claimed to have special
knowledge that would enhance Christian experience. The
other group were the Judaizers who tried to enforce conform-
ity of Christians to the Jewish ceremonial law.

I wonder if we are clear about what this foundation is? What
do we know about it? Based upon this verse there are a number
of things.

A predetermined foundation.

It was forecast by the prophets.

See, I lay a stone in Zion, a tested stone, a precious cornerstone for a sure foundation (Isaiah 28:16).

He has set his foundation on the holy mountain; the LORD loves the gates of Zion ... Glorious things are said of you, O city of God (Psalm 87: 1-3).

The prophets had a glimpse of that foundation and were 'trying to find out the times and circumstances to which the Spirit of Christ in them was pointing when he predicted the sufferings of Christ and the glories that would follow' (1 Peter 1:11).

In fact, long before the prophets ever came along, long before God caused creation to appear, it was *fixed by predestination*.

For you know that it was not with perishable things such as silver or gold that you were redeemed from the empty way of life handed down to you from your forefathers, but with the precious blood of Christ, a lamb without blemish or defect. He was chosen from before the creation of the world, but was revealed in these last times for your sake (1 Peter 1:18-20).

Peter says that foundation was predestined; the Lamb that takes away the sin of the world, who died on the cross was slain from the foundation of the world. What happened at Calvary, two thousand years ago, was simply the following of a blueprint that had been predestined in eternity. And only a fool would try to change that in the closing decade of the 20th century.

The foundation was also *founded by preaching*.

Paul, a servant of God and an apostle of Jesus Christ, for the faith of God's elect and the knowledge of the truth that leads to godliness - a faith and knowledge resting on the hope of eternal life, which God, who does not lie, promised before the beginning of time, and at his appointed season he brought his word to light through the preaching entrusted to me by the command of God our Saviour (Titus 1:1-3).

A provided foundation

It is provided, or as Jude puts it '...the faith that was once for all entrusted to the saints' (Jude 3). We do not need to go looking for this blueprint in an archives building as though no one knows what the faith is. We have got it in the Bible, given by inspiration of God. The Bible is the architectural blueprint, not only for the foundation, but also as we will see in later chapters for the superstructure.

Yet I see an ominous trend today in some places. I do not mean to be unfair and to take some shots at some places where I think God is doing a work, but I see a trend where some who are very zealous for the Lord, are more interested in, I can only call it, *existential prophecy*, than they are in learning the Bible. They will spend time together, hoping that somebody will utter a word, a prophecy, and that is what they come for. It is far easier just to let somebody stand up and say, 'Thus says the Lord and here goes...' and you give some kind of word and people say, 'Well, God spoke to me.' That may happen, but I fear it is often motivated by an undisciplined attempt to by-pass the study of the provided foundation - the Bible.

A precise foundation

This was revealed to certain select people in the early church. Those whom God chose, including the great apostle Paul, though he was one of the greatest intellects in the history of the world, were not allowed to do their own thing: 'I did not receive it from any man, nor was I taught it; rather, I received it by revelation from Jesus Christ' (Galatians 1:12). John wrote, 'That ... which we have heard, which we have seen with our eyes ... we proclaim' (1 John 1:1,2). The disciples, in Acts 4:20 said: 'For we cannot help speaking about what we have seen and heard'.

But that is not all: this preciseness is revealed in the fact that while it is restricted yet it can be constructed on:

Built on the foundation of the apostles and prophets, with
Christ Jesus himself as the chief cornerstone (Ephesians 2:20).

I don't believe that we can improve upon a statement made
by somebody in the nineteenth century, I'm not exactly sure
who it was: 'Where the Scriptures speak, we speak. Where the
Scriptures are silent, we are silent.' But where we know what
has been revealed and what we have received there is precision
and we are not afraid to speak.

A permanent foundation

This foundation is an unchangeable foundation, not just from
place to place as in Ephesus or Corinth or Thessalonica, but
also from generation to generation. This is why Jude says '...I
urge you to contend for the faith that was once for all entrusted
to the saints'. It is not received *from* the saints, it is delivered
to the saints.

This is why you should be able to go anywhere in Britain (or
anywhere in the world) and find the same foundation. You may
not like the tradition; you may not like the way they carry out their
order of worship; you may not like it if it is very liturgical; or you
may not like it if it is very open with a free style of worship.
Similarly, you may find that there are various idiosyncrasies in
superstructures, but you should find the same foundation wherever you go. It is not only unchangeable, it is unique because this
foundation is literally a person who died and was raised from the
dead and ascended to heaven where he took his place at the right
hand of God from where he sent the Spirit down to the church.

A perfect foundation

There is not a flaw in what God has devised: his blueprint is
perfect. I would remind you that God has a blueprint for your
own life. If you want to be a fool, you can tamper with those

plans and say, 'I want this which God has not included to be in his plan,' and you can write it in. But remember, what he has conceived for you and the way you should live your life, sixty seconds a minute, every minute of every day, is best.

A preaching foundation

I have already said it was founded in preaching. It 'pleased God by the foolishness of preaching to save them that believe'. I fear for any church not based upon preaching. The foundation may be the boring part. There is nothing particularly attractive about a foundation but if that foundation is not right, then the superstructure will be worthless.

There are people today who want short cuts and quick ways to get blessings from God. As soon as they are converted they think they are going to know more than anybody. They talk about being filled with the Spirit (I am not making fun of that because I am not anti-charismatic). But you can spend time hoping for prophecy and signs and wonders, and ten years later still be pursuing the same path, and although God may fill you with his Spirit, you will still be empty-headed.

Jesus promised that when the Spirit would come he would bring to our remembrance what Jesus said. You need to take time to read your Bible, to engage in Bible study and to read helpful books.

A persecuted foundation

The devil does not care how he can undermine the foundation; he will try to bring it through what may be called today, liberalism, or he will try to do it through legalism, as the Judaizers wanted to do. Either way Jesus Christ is put to one side. Jesus did not fit into the plans of the Jews, and was put to one side. As the foundation was persecuted then, so we can expect it to be now.

A propitious foundation

This perhaps is the main thing that the apostle Paul would want to be said about this foundation. Why do I use the word 'propitious'? You could say because it begins with the letter 'P'! But if I was only going to choose one word it would be this one.

> But if anybody does sin, we have one who speaks to the Father in our defence - Jesus Christ, the Righteous One. He is the atoning sacrifice (propitiation) for our sins... (1 John 2:1,2).

What does John mean? For God to be propitious toward us means that he is favourable toward us, because when Jesus died he *was* the propitiation who satisfied the justice of God! Thus calling this foundation propitious simply means that all who rest on it are saved. The superstructure may go wrong but all who rest upon the foundation are saved.

Do you know that you are saved? There is something infinitely worse than being saved by fire at the judgment seat of Christ: not to be saved at all and be eternally lost. To put it another way; there is something far worse than receiving no reward at the judgment seat of Christ: to miss Heaven altogether and be sent to Hell.

5

A Lasting Superstructure

If any man builds on this foundation using gold, silver, costly stones, wood, hay or straw (1 Corinthians 3:12).

In the last chapter we looked at the foundation, now we turn to the superstructure and find Paul revealing the inseparable connection between the superstructure and our reward at the judgment seat of Christ.

He introduced this first in verse 8 of this chapter: 'each will be *rewarded* according to his own labour'. He uses the word 'reward' again in verse 14: 'If what he has built survives, he will receive his reward'. In between these verses he shows *how that superstructure will be judged*.

In 2 Corinthians 5:10 Paul elaborates on this. He writes:

For we must all appear before the judgment seat of Christ, that each one may receive what is due to him for the things done while in the body, whether good or bad.

Some would like to think, simply because they are saved and are justified by Christ's blood through faith, that following the judgment there will only be either Heaven or Hell, and that is all there is. But that is not the whole story. Salvation is what God gives us for believing in Jesus, the foundation on which we build. But reward is a New Testament teaching that is closely connected to the future inheritance of Christians.

In Colossians 3:24 Paul wrote, '... since you know that you will receive an inheritance from the Lord as a reward.' There he actually says inheritance is reward. Actually my friend, Dr Michael Eaton, made his doctoral study largely on this, and he is convinced that every time the word *inheritance* is used, it refers to reward. Sometimes instead of reward, it will be the word, crown; sometimes it is the word, prize.

I do think though that we need to see the superstructure at two levels, and I want to talk about the church's superstructure first.

The church's superstructure

(i) teaching

The teaching of the church is a reflection of the whole church's superstructure. Because of this we need to know whether the church's teaching ministry is biblical or biased.

I dare say that there are preachers who are so biased with certain themes that whenever they preach it will always be the same message. I have a friend whose sermons I like to hear but I know before I hear them I am going to get the five points of Calvinism. The superstructure of his ministry reflects that. His teaching is very biblical incidentally. I do not disagree with most of what I hear, but it is biased, and therefore not balanced. The one advantage of expository preaching when you go through the Scripture is that you let the text give the agenda for what one preaches.

(ii) tradition

Tradition can be good and it can be bad. Similarly it can be indifferent. It is made up of three things: provincialism, denominationalism and style of leadership.

Provincialism sometimes is called parochialism. Generally speaking, it would refer to one's national culture and where one lives. Eastern Christianity and western Christianity have their own traditions and within western Christianity there can be, for example, British cultural influences or American cultural influences. Then, in particular, the smaller a provincial church is, the more parochial it will probably be, because a smaller church will usually reflect an immediate area of the same class, neighbourhood, colour and so forth, and that is unavoidable.

Tradition is also bound up with denominationalism: Church of England, Non-Conformist, Baptist, Methodist, the superstructure will reflect one's denominational preference. Theological emphasis will be seen in the superstructure: the church's ecclesiology, its doctrine of the church, its view of the Lord's Supper, its style of worship and many other distinctions.

Style of leadership is also important in the formation of tradition. Often the leader's personality will be mirrored in the people. Take, for instance, a denomination that begins under a strong man. It is very interesting to see how that denomination will, for years, maybe generations, reflect the style of leadership of that one man who started it. Many of his eccentricities will be filtered right down into the people. Similarly you can often tell whether a person is a Baptist, Methodist or Brethren without him telling you so, if you talk to him for a while. It goes back to leadership and as with tradition this can be good, it can be bad, it can be indifferent. The point I am making here is that tradition is unavoidable.

(iii) time
It is a melancholy fact that most superstructures do not improve with time. Most churches grow cold, complacent, and often liberal over the years. Very few churches, having gone off the rails, return to a warm evangelical heart. Time reveals

whether the superstructure dignifies its foundation. For example, how it reacts to change, general trends and conditions, changes of ministers and members within show this up.

The church's superstructure - teaching, tradition, time - will have to pass the fiery test too! How much teaching is wood, hay, straw? How much tradition? What has passing of time done to deteriorate the church's superstructure? These questions haunt me as a church leader. We cannot forget that one day the truth of your church and mine will be out in the open for all to see. The Day will declare it!

The believer's own superstructure

Notice how he puts it: 'If any man builds on this foundation.' Paul, in using the words, 'if any' is looking at every member of the church at Corinth individually, one by one, and we need to look at ourselves in this way without looking at anyone else. The first thing I want to deal with is why he chooses these particular metaphors: gold, silver, costly stones.

(i) viability

Something is viable according to its 'survival probability'. The reason Paul uses this metaphor of gold, silver and costly stones is because he is dealing with the question of whether the superstructure will survive fire. In other words, will it last? Gold, silver and costly stones survive fire. Wood, hay and straw will be burned up. So the question is, will your superstructure survive? Is it viable?

(ii) virtue

Paul is after *virtue*, excellence. Gold, silver and costly stones are set against things that are superficial, shallow, worthless - wood, hay, straw. So translating this into the spiritual realm: virtue means goodness, genuineness, moral excellence.

(iii) visibility
The superstructure is a thing to be seen. If it is gold, silver,
costly stones, it will be a thing of visible beauty. God wants to
turn us into a likeness of Jesus Christ, that we might be refined,
polished, and something of beauty.

(iv) variety
He does not name one precious stone or gem but his list
includes many: gold, silver, costly gems. We have all got
various gifts. Each can make his own contribution. We all, I
hope, manifest the fruit of the Spirit, and there is variety here.
There is variety in this thing of beauty.

(v) value
However, I think the main reason Paul has chosen gold, silver
and costly stones as the metaphors he would use to show the
superstructure, is that they have value. Gold, silver and costly
stones have value opposed to wood, hay and straw. The
question then is, When does value show itself to be such?

First, in the here and now. Paul said to Timothy:

> In a large house there are articles not only of gold and silver,
> but also of wood and clay; some are for noble purposes and
> some for ignoble. If a man cleanses himself from the latter,
> he will be an instrument for noble purposes, made holy,
> useful to the Master and prepared to do any good work (2
> Timothy 2:20,21).

We can be valuable right now for if this teaching will be
accepted and applied, it will make a difference in all our lives.

But not only will it be valuable now, it will be valuable at
the judgment seat of Christ, and you will be glad that you built
upon that foundation (which assures you of eternal salvation),

a superstructure of gold, silver and costly stones.

What am I made of?

The crucial question is: how do we know whether our own individual superstructure is comprised of gold, silver and costly stones?

First, our *application of teaching*. We must first understand it. Then we must receive it for ourselves. Thereafter, we must make it change us.

Secondly, our *approach to temptation*. What do we do when we are tempted? Maybe we are going to face real temptation but it is up to us whether we resist it or succumb to it.

Thirdly, our *attitude toward trial*. We cannot avoid trial. Jesus said, 'In this world you will have trouble' (John 16:33). As Christians we will face trouble and trial, perhaps even worse than we have known before. Our attitude toward trial will often largely determine whether gold, silver and costly stones comprise our superstructure or whether it is wood, hay and straw. You can look at trial as God's invitation on a silver platter to move up higher; or you can discredit it, show contempt for the trial and after it is over be no better off because you refused to dignify it.

There is a fourth way of finding out what you are made of and it is probably the main one: our *ability with the tongue*. In Matthew 12:36-37, Jesus described the day of judgment:

> But I tell you that men will have to give account on the day of judgment for every careless word they have spoken. For by your words you will be acquitted, and by your words you will be condemned.

That does not refer to whether you are saved or lost, because in the context the person has already been assumed to be saved.

Here he is talking about our words. What you and I actually *say* will in all probability be what gets us into trouble and will grieve the Holy Spirit.

> Likewise the tongue is a small part of the body, but it makes great boasts. Consider what a great forest is set on fire by a small spark (James 3:5).

Did you ever read this verse in Proverbs 10:19: 'When words are many, sin is not absent'. I guarantee you: gold, silver and costly stones will be our own superstructure largely to the degree to which you and I control our tongues.

6

Tongues of Straw

His work will be shown for what it is (1 Corinthians 3:13)

The work to which this verse refers is the superstructure and as we discussed at the close of the previous chapter, we build that superstructure partly by our *words*. To the extent we control the tongue, that superstructure will be made up of gold, silver, costly stones; to the extent that we manifest intemperate talk, it will be a superstructure of wood, hay and straw.

Intemperate talk
We get a little closer to the bone when we look at how the Christian can erect a superstructure of wood, hay and straw by intemperate talk.

In 2 Corinthians 5:10 Paul points out the link between our *deeds* and the judgment seat of Christ. He writes:

> For we must all appear before the judgment seat of Christ, that each one may receive what is due to him for the things done while in the body, whether good or bad.

Jesus showed us that our words play no small part in this when he said, '...men will have to give account on the day of judgment for every careless word they have spoken'.

The word, *careless*, comes from a Greek word that means, *unemployed*. It means, up to no good. It is used in Matthew 20:6 in the parable of the vineyard: 'Why have you been

standing here all day long doing *nothing*?' It is a word that
means, useless, unserviceable, incapable of good. It is translated *unproductive* in 2 Peter 1:8: 'For if you possess these
qualities in increasing measure, they will keep you from being
ineffective and unproductive in your knowledge of our Lord
Jesus Christ'. Our words that are up to no good, that are barren
or unproductive, we will give an account of at the judgment.

Cheap talk

To develop this further look at Romans 14:10:

> You, then, why do you judge your brother? Or why do you
> look down on your brother? For we will all stand before
> God's judgment seat.

There is an inseparable link between our words and the
judgment. Indeed, how do we judge people? It is by words.

If I want to destroy someone's reputation to you, I can use
a few cheap words, and I have set that person at nought.

What Talk Will Be Revealed Then?

There are five things concerning the use of our tongues that
will come out at the judgment seat of Christ.

(i) validity of our concerns.

Every man's concern will be made manifest. A good way of
testing this is to ask, what is it we talk about most? Jesus said
in Matthew 12:34: 'For out of the overflow of the heart the
mouth speaks'. Our talk reveals what we are. Our talk is an
index into what really matters to us. How much of your talk
really is about the Lord even to fellow-Christians? To put it
another way: what is it you want most in all the world? Your
goals, your dreams, your plans, your aims. That day will reveal
the validity of your concerns.

(ii) validity of our counsel

I see two aspects: first, the counsel you have received and taken on board; and second, the counsel you have given.

No doubt you will make decisions based upon what people told you that you ought to do for in much counsel there is safety. But suppose you got bad counsel? Will you be able to blame that person at the judgment seat of Christ? Notice 2 John 8: 'Watch out that you do not lose what you have worked for, but that you may be rewarded fully'. It is possible for you to take on *board counsel that could destroy* your own superstructure.

But that is not all. If you have given unwise counsel and it was accepted, that person will have to answer for himself. But how will you feel in that day when the fire proves the validity of your counsel? I will have to give an account of the counsel I have given from the pulpit and in the vestry. I pray, 'God, don't let me say anything wrong that will lead this person in the wrong direction.' For in that Day the counsel you and I have given to others will be brought into the open.

(iii) validity of our claims

This will come out in that Day and can be described under three categories: the validity of our theological claims; second, of our personal claims; and third, our spiritual claims.

Our theological claims

This probably means a little more to me than to some of you. I am a theologian - one of my professors of my old seminary called me 'a theological animal' and I took it as a compliment. I love theology, it is perhaps something I think of more than most and therefore it may affect me more than some of you.

Speaking personally, I have taken a strong stand for what I believe. Not everybody agrees with me. In that Day my mouth will be stopped. Now I can build my case and put forward chapter and verse, logic and rhetoric, but then I'll have to lower my voice and wait and hear the verdict, for the undoubted truth will be brought to light.

Our personal claims
Jesus speaks of this in Luke 14:7ff.

> When he noticed how the guests picked the places of honour at the table, he told them this parable: "When someone invites you to a wedding feast, do not take the place of honour, for a person more distinguished than you may have been invited. If so, the host who invited both of you, will come and say to you, 'Give this man your seat.' Then, humiliated, you will have to take the least important place. But when you are invited, take the lowest place so that when your host comes, he will say to you, 'Friend, move up to a better place.' Then you will be honoured in the presence of all your fellow-guests. For everyone who exalts himself will be humbled, and he who humbles himself will be exalted."

I regard that parable as having very considerable application for this aspect of the judgment. It is because in that Day it will all be clear what is the truth. In the meantime, we can make claims and be like the foolish person who went and sat at the top table, but in that Day it will all come out. Perhaps you want people to think you are so brilliant and knowledgeable: we will find out then just how little you know! Your claim to integrity and how your integrity has been impugned, and how you feel that you have been walked over and that you deserve vindication will all be seen in the light of truth.

If you deserve vindication you are going to get it. If you have been abused, lied about, hurt, mistreated and you are the victim of injustice, God does not like it and he is going to vindicate you. He might do it in this life - he can do it - but there are no promises that he will. All the promises of vindication refer to the final judgment. And so your personal claims will be proved valid or invalid on that Day.

Our spiritual claims

What about spiritual claims? This means how spiritual we really were. You will find out then how spiritual I really was. How much one really has prayed, tithed, worked, got involved, cared - all out in the open. Paul says, 'His work will be shown for what it is because the Day' (and I like the way the NIV capitalises the word, Day), 'the Day will bring it to light'.

(iv) validity of our criticisms

I move to the fourth thing: the validity of our criticisms. It will all be out in the open: all our personal judgments will be laid bare. Are you a particular person who finds it easy to criticise? Would you say that you have a reputation for being judgmental? We will find out how right you were to find fault with everybody and everything, because the validity of your criticisms will be out in the open. All personal judgments will be laid bare including what you have said to others in cutting them down. We will all get to see how you did it. What you did privately to a person and left them in tears, will be revealed to all.

It will be quite a day. Every idle word spoken we will give an account of. However, if God deals with us now concerning our wrong words, and we confess it, because we are really sorry and we put right the matter, we can be spared then. All our wrong words can be burned by the fire of chastening now, so that all the things that have been said about this person or that person will not be revealed. There may be cases for us having to go to a particular person and say, 'I'm sorry'; there is a place for restitution for if that is not done, there was not real repentance. I think we all know when we have to do it.

(v) validity of our complaints

Finally, what I want to consider is whether you have a complaint and, if so, is it valid? God knows whether it is valid. Do you feel that it has been unfair that you have had to live all these years with that particular man? Or do you think that God has not been fair to you because you never married, and you have complained? Do you have a valid complaint? It may be. God knows whether it is.

But let me ask you this, in your complaining do you roll up your sleeves or do you let God handle it? The one thing that can be said about the judgment that must never be underestimated is that it will be the day when God is going to clear his name and that justice will be carried out totally and in an undoubted way. God knows what people have said. God knows how the infidel shakes his fist, and says, 'If there's a God why does he let this happen?' God can wait.

But that will be a day when he will be involved. Judgment will be carried out by an all-wise and all-righteous God who has a perfect memory of everything that ever happened. His Day can be your day, but if you make today, your day and do not wait for his Day, then that comes under a different category, what the Bible calls 'grumbling'. In 1 Corinthians 10:10 Paul, referring to the children of Israel, says: 'And do not grumble, as some of them did - and were killed by the destroying angel'. You ought to know that grumbling is put alongside three other sins: idolatry (v7); sexual immorality (v8); testing God (v9).

We will be judged not only on what we have done, then, but also on what we have said. Indignation may have led you to complain but we must always ask ourselves, do we speak with tongues of gold, or tongues of straw?

7

Building The Wrong Superstructure

If any man builds on this foundation using gold, silver, costly stones, wood, hay or straw (1 Corinthians 3:12).

With regard to the foundation, there are three assumptions. The first is that all those who build upon this foundation are already true Christians. The second is that all Christians will build upon this foundation in some way or another. The third assumption is that the choice of materials determines whether the superstructure will last. If it is made of gold, silver and costly stones, then it will survive; but if it is made of wood, hay, or straw, it will not survive for the fire will burn it up at the last day.

In an earlier chapter we looked at the first three, which go together: gold, silver and costly stones, the lasting superstructure. In this chapter we are going to look at the second part of that verse: wood, hay and straw. We are going to focus on the awesome, fearful possibility of erecting a superstructure from these materials which make it faulty from the first stone that is laid.

Two erroneous interpretations of this verse
There are those who interpret the wood, hay, straw as metaphors to describe false professions. They say, for example, that an evangelist may see many people profess faith but possibly not all of those people are saved. What about those

who profess faith falsely and therefore are not saved? His converts will be burned up. In other words, according to this interpretation, his work, which is a metaphor to describe his converts, will be destroyed because they were never saved. Thus the evangelist, himself, will be saved but his efforts will be destroyed. But this interpretation puts the responsibility upon the preacher, not the ordinary Christian or even those who profess falsely.

Another way it is interpreted is this: that the wood, hay, straw are metaphors that depict odd doctrine or strange, alien teaching. There may be, it is claimed, a minister who himself is a Christian but teaches screwy ideas and a lot of people believe and repeat them and heresies develop as a result. The idea is that the teaching will be burned up but the teacher will be saved. This again would put the responsibility upon the teacher, not the ordinary Christian, much less the misguided.

What are we to say about these ideas? Neither view would fit Paul's purpose of rebuking carnal Christians for their carelessness and for their childishness.

Why *would* a true Christian be so stupid as to build a superficial superstructure? How could it happen? Let me mention three possibilities although there are more.

Builders in wood, hay and straw

The first of these builders is the person *caught in a sin*. In Galatians 6:1 Paul says: 'Brothers, if someone is caught in a sin, you who are spiritual should restore him gently. But watch yourself, or you also may be tempted.' A Christian can therefore be caught in a sin, or overtaken in a fault. Why does Paul say, 'restore him gently'? Because the man caught in a sin was a converted person. You cannot restore someone who has not been saved. There is one reason you would try and restore a person like that, and that is he is a backslider. But he is a Christian.

A second example of how a Christian can build a super-structure of wood, hay and straw is the result of *faulty teaching*. Not all Christians get good teaching and in a sense they cannot help it. But their superstructure is worthless.

There is a third possibility and that is when one *does not heed the warning of external chastening*, which I described in a previous chapter.

The metaphors

Let me just explain why Paul chose metaphors of wood, hay and straw in this connection.

He wanted to pick metaphors that show *corruptibility* - wood, hay, straw are capable of decay, of rot, of uselessness, particularly compared to gold, silver and costly stones.

He wanted to pick that which would show *colourlessness*; that would be unattractive as a superstructure, as opposed to gold, silver, costly stones.

The metaphors are also effective in illustrating what is *commonplace*, what is available anywhere, what is convenient, what you do not have to look very far to find. You can find these anywhere as opposed to what is rare - gold, silver, costly stones.

He chose these metaphors also because he wanted to show what is *cheap*, of little worth; against gold, silver and costly stones.

And he wanted to show what is *combustible*. Wood, hay and straw, as opposed to gold, silver, costly stones, will not survive the final test in that Day.

Personal responsibility

Paul continues in verses 12 and 13: 'If any man builds *on* this foundation' - the foundation being Christ's work and that for which we can take no credit because by grace we have been incorporated into the foundation. Undoubtedly we are in

Christ by free and sovereign grace, and so that is not by works, that is by grace alone. But the superstructure is one's own work. Notice how Paul says: 'If any man *builds* on this foundation using gold, silver, costly stones, wood, hay or straw, his *work* will be shown for what it is, because the Day will bring it to light' – a reference to the judgment seat of Christ, 'because it shall be revealed by fire; and the fire shall try every man's work of what sort it is.'

It is important then as part of our responsibility to identify these base materials in our superstructure. We must ask what sort of work will be burned up at the judgment seat of Christ? How can we recognise it so that we can be duly warned?

Incongruous teaching
The first evidence which we can identify refers to the church collectively – but I want to see how it affects individuals – and that is *incongruous teaching*. Now what precisely is this? It is teaching that is unbecoming to the foundation. There are various examples of this and I would have to say that Arminianism is a superstructure of wood, hay, straw.

(i) Arminianism
Arminianism is the belief that denies the doctrine of election and purports a person can lose their salvation even though they have been truly converted. Although Arminius stood against John Calvin's teaching of election and predestination, I believe that Arminius himself was a Christian just as I believe that there are many Arminians who are Christians. Yet to deny the doctrine of election is to erect a superstructure that is incongruous. It does not dignify the foundation because we have been put into the foundation by free and sovereign grace. Paul has been teaching that from the beginning of this letter. What about people who deny the teaching 'once saved, always

saved'? The irony is that they are still saved. They may not know it now but they will find out when they get to heaven, that they did not need to worry all those years for they were saved once and for all. But that is not the only example of incongruous teaching.

(ii) *Antinomianism*

This is the denial of law: it is lawlessness, an architectural plan for ungodly living. It is sometimes called, hyper-Calvinism. It is the abuse of free grace. I have friends whom I can only call hyper-Calvinists. I have actually heard them say that because believers are in Christ, their sins are forgiven, past, present and future, and that it does not matter what they do, they do not need to worry about this business of reward. They cite the parable of the vineyard (Matthew 20:1-16), where the one who came in at the eleventh hour received the same pay as the one who worked all day long.

I have watched what that teaching does. In too many cases where people did not even feel a need to live a holy life because they say, 'We know we are saved, we know we have an interest in Christ,' there is just a carelessness in their own personal lives. They say, 'Never mind this talk about rewards; it does not add dignity to the sovereign grace of God if you talk about rewards. All will be equally saved; all will be equally rewarded.' I call that a subtle, if not a blatant form of Antinomianism. Not all who would hold that view are Antinomians but I have seen it so often.

(iii) *Liberalism*

By Liberalism, I am referring to an example of one who, although converted, later on for whatever reason, through a bad influence, for example, goes to a liberal seminary, reads the higher critics and leaves his evangelical heritage. I am not saying all liberals are saved because many of them are apostates, as described in 2 Peter 2 and the Epistle of Jude. But I am saying that it is possible for somebody to get off the rails, theologically. You may say, 'Well, I don't know how anybody could believe that today.' But there are people today in the ministry, and I believe they have been converted, but because they have listened to what they were taught at university or seminary, they are never the same again. But they will be saved.

(iv) *Legalism*

This is the fourth thing that I put under the head of incongruous teaching. The Legalists are Christians who bring in the law as a condition for whether you are Christian. That was the error of the churches in Galatia. Paul grieved over these churches. It was not a case of Antinomianism getting in; as far as we know it was a case of bringing in the law. The Galatians were taught a false introspection that they were saved by their reverence to the law. Paul says, 'Thinking that means that they are cut off from Christ.' It did not mean that they had lost their salvation but they had *cut the supply of grace* and had become legalistic and introspective. I think some Puritans, though not all of them, did this. In the words of Jim Packer, they became more interested in godliness than God, and introspection becomes a bondage. But they will be saved. That is what I mean by incongruous teaching.

Intrusive traditions

This is a second evidence of erecting wood, hay and straw and it is taking incongruous teaching a step further. In an earlier chapter I referred to tradition as being either good, bad or indifferent. Sometimes a new Christian will adopt the traditions not knowing there may be something wrong with them. You may say, 'It is impossible to be converted in a church that has a bad tradition.' But do not be so sure. God can use a crooked stick to draw a straight line and it is amazing how you run into people who were converted in a place you would never have thought it possible. Yet there are those that are never able to separate tradition from Scripture.

It is sad to say but in 1545, the Council of Trent, the commission called by the Roman Catholic Church, said Scripture is equal to tradition. They simply made official what had long been the practice. This is why God raised up the Protestant Reformers like Luther, Calvin and Zwingli. But that did not mean everybody in the Roman Catholic church was not saved. There are a lot of Roman Catholics, alive today, that will be in heaven. I can tell you this, never think a person cannot be a Christian merely because he has accepted an intrusive tradition, because there are also legalistic Christians in the church today, and in the sight of God it may be that legalism is as obnoxious as the Mass!

But legalism may not bother you because you are sort of at home with it. But you need to know that there will be a lot of people in heaven. They will come from the House Church Movement, they will come from Pentecostal churches, they will come from Brethren assemblies. There will be Calvinists in heaven and there will be Southern Baptists in heaven.

I suspect many of us have far more wood, hay and straw in our superstructure than we would like to admit. We are all incorporated into that foundation by sheer grace. Remember that a sovereign God has his elect in a variety of places, for instance not all of God's elect in the United Kingdom are converted by those who are perfectly right theologically. Otherwise no one would be saved! We all want to think that we have got it right. I hope I have! But I dare say that there is a lot in R T Kendall's thinking that needs correcting. I hope to get it right before I get to heaven. What if I don't? God has a way of withholding certain insights and sharing them with others to keep us all humble. But he will have all the glory for at the judgment seat of Christ we will all lower our voices.

Lifestyle
I will suggest five types of lifestyle that I believe show how a Christian can erect this superstructure of wood, hay or straw.

(i) Smugness
We can recognise smugness in other people although seldom can we see it in ourselves; yet it is one of those things that is hard to prove. I believe that the word that most accurately depicts British evangelicalism at the present time is smugness. You find it wherever you go, whether you are with a group of ministers, or a larger gathering, whether it is denominational, or involving other denominations, they all believe that they are the ones that have got it right: 'We are the ones God is blessing, we are saying this, this, this...' Where is that one who will say, 'There is something wrong with *us*!'

In order not to have to listen to what God may be saying through someone else, we justify ourselves as being the ones that God is going to work through; if blessing comes, it will come through us! We do not like to think that God could be doing a work somewhere else with someone of whom we do not approve. Our attitudes betray that we are the ones 'rich, and increased with goods, who have need of nothing' (Revelation 3:17 AV). But really we are talking about self-satisfaction, which is basically self-righteousness. Do you know that self-righteous people are the hardest people in the world to reach?

I would rather deal with anybody rather than a self-righteous Christian. I have begun praying, 'God save *me* from self-righteousness'. It is the easiest trait in the world to come into my own life when I literally think it is all right with me, it is the other person that is in the wrong.

I would much rather deal with a person who has been overtaken by sexual sin or the sin of gossip or the sin of greed. When you are dealing with a self-righteous person you have a battle on your hands. And this is why smugness is so dangerous.

Perhaps you do not like this teaching. But if this sounds like you, then if you go on that way I guarantee you, one day your superstructure of smugness will come out. The truth is that smug people have no objectivity about themselves; they live in a dream world. They do not think for they know they are right!

The rule of thumb therefore is stay smug and you will erect a superstructure of straw. Be broken and you will erect a superstructure of gold.

(ii) Tension

This second characteristic is found in the person who is tense, uptight, with no peace within himself. I am talking about the Christian who can be very involved in the work of God; we can talk about a minister, minister's wife, deacon, deacon's wife, church member, someone very involved. But that person can be a busybody, is uptight, sometimes makes others perfectly miserable. They are always past masters at judging others. Instead of giving a feeling of warmth and liberty they give people 'the creeps' and create tension.

This person has no liberty in himself. The Bible says 'where the Spirit of the Lord is, there is freedom' (2 Corinthians 3:17). They are irritable and that irritability is always just a quarter of an inch beneath the surface. Anything can cause it to be manifest.

Often a person like this is very high in his doctrine on the sovereignty of God, but is the first to panic and complain when something goes wrong. Why? Because their doctrine of the sovereignty of God will not be sufficient to develop a transparent lifestyle, if they do not control the tongue. Years of an intemperate tongue result in inconsistent traits, so that person is a complainer, a grumbler who hasn't learned to dignify the trial; and a lifestyle of grumbling is the result. It comes out in the superstructure.

The second rule of thumb is stay judgmental and you will erect a superstructure of straw. But if you come to have peace within yourself and let things be, you will erect a superstructure of gold.

(iii) Revenge

Thirdly, some Christians live to 'get even'. They feel hurt all the time, and all they think about is the day they can get even. Now, sometimes there is a natural if not understandable explanation. Sometimes a person like this has been deeply hurt even as a child, and they have damaged emotions. Or perhaps this person has been abused or lied about or put down. He feels mistreated and so even though he is a Christian, there is this unconscious anger with which he has not come to terms though he is saved and will go to heaven when he dies – his lifestyle is one of determination to prove himself. He cannot forgive others, he holds a grudge and lives for one thing – vindication. For those of us who are like this, God is always too slow in dealing with things, so we take things into our own hands.

Rule of thumb number three: get even now and you will erect a superstructure of straw. Let God handle it and you will erect a superstructure of gold.

(iv) Affectation

Fourthly there is the lifestyle of affectation. Yes, there are Christians like this. They are really saved, but who are just, I can only call them, superficial. They really want, most of all, to impress others, either by their clothes or by their accent or by whom they know. What really pleases them is to make others feel a bit jealous! They want to see somebody envy them. Nothing makes them feel better than that.

People like this are often social climbers; they want to be seen with the right people and they choose the church that will make them look good. People like this are haughty, arrogant and they make others feel inferior. Often people like this are racially prejudiced. You often see among some of them an inverted snobbery: they do not want to dress too smart because it is really up-market not to look too great. It is the very opposite to the way Jesus is.

The fourth rule of thumb therefore is make people admire you and you will erect a superstructure of straw. Be content with the honour that comes from God only and yours will be a superstructure of gold.

(v) Worldliness

Fifthly, there are Christians who are marked by worldliness. 1 John 2:15-16 is very specific in its denunciation of worldliness,

> Do not love the world or anything in the world. If anyone loves the world, the love of the Father is not in him. For everything in the world - the cravings of sinful man, the lust of his eyes and the boasting of what he has and does - comes not from the Father but from the world.

I believe worldliness comes down to three things: sensuality, sophistication and secularisation.

Sensuality is the lust of the flesh: people obsessed with sex, as opposed to a lifestyle of self-denial. *Sophistication* can be thought of as the lust of the eyes: people obsessed with culture, learning and refinement as opposed to simplicity. *Secularisation* - John calls it 'the pride of life' - is the obsession with material things, as opposed to spirituality.

Worldly Christians who would rather stay home and watch television on Sunday night are nevertheless often the first to criticise things. They appear godly and righteous when they are in fact hypocrites.

This is why Christians do not tithe! They can look for every reason in the world why they should not have to do it. It is the worldly spirit that looks for a way not to tithe.

This is why they do not pray. I was talking to someone not long ago whose marriage is on the rocks. I just said to them, 'How much do each of you pray?' I was not surprised to hear, not at all. How much time *do* we spend in prayer, by ourselves? How much time do *you* take to be alone with God? Thirty minutes a day should be the minimum for each of us. I do not care how busy we are. It will give me no pleasure to stand beside you at the judgment seat of Christ and watch a videotape of these words being flashed before you, when in fact you justified how busy you were at the time.

Rule of thumb number five: get immediate gratification because you want to enjoy the things of the world now and you will erect a superstructure of straw; but if you have the love of the Father in you, it will be a superstructure of gold.

Breaking the bad habits
This kind of lifestyle is not developed in a day, it takes years. You may say, 'It is too late for me.' But if it were too late, God would not have me write this! It is never too late!

I think of Archbishop Cranmer who vacillated so much between Rome and Canterbury. Finally he came out on the side against Rome on the subject of the Eucharist. In a weak moment, however, he signed a recantation saying that he was sorry for having views of the Lord's Supper that displeased Rome, but they burned him at the stake anyway. He must have felt pretty awful, used, wondering what it was worth. But do you know what he did? When they burned him at the stake and the flames came up, the first thing he did was to put that hand that had signed the recantation into the fire, sending a signal to the world that he was sorry. And it turned out to be his finest hour. There was still time even for him.

I think of Samson, who was so foolish when Delilah captivated his heart that he was never the same again. Yet we are told that in his last moment the number of Israel's enemies which he slew at his death were more than those which he slew in his life. At the very last moment God used him.

A mixed superstructure

One further clarification is in order. Have you ever noticed that there is no little word, *or*, in verse 12. The NIV throws in an *or*, before 'straw' because they think it will make it read better, but verse 12 says: 'If any man builds on this foundation using gold, silver, costly stones, wood, hay, straw' - no *or* - he didn't say, gold, silver, costly stones or wood, hay or straw. There is no *or*. Why? It will be a multiple superstructure. There will be varying degrees of value in the same superstructure. It will be a mixed superstructure; it will include *both* valuable and worthless materials.

It is not a question therefore whether you will either have a superstructure of gold, silver, costly stones, or the other having wood, hay, straw, but it will be mixed. And there is a bit of the wood, the hay and the straw in the best of God's saints. Because James said, in James 3:2, 'If anyone is never at fault in what he says, he is a perfect man'.

And so with us, none of us is perfect, we have all sinned, but it is not too late. God is gracious and we can begin now to develop a transparent character that will be translated into gold, silver, costly stones. And we will be glad, one day, that we did.

8

God's Day

His work will be shown for it is, because the Day will bring
it to light. It will be revealed with fire, and the fire will test
the quality of each man's work (1 Corinthians 3:13).

In this chapter we shall look mainly at one word, the three-
letter word, 'day'. The NIV gives it a capital D - '...the Day
shall bring it to light'. Paul felt no need to explain what he
meant by that 'Day'. It was so obvious. Elsewhere he would
say 'the day of Christ Jesus' (Philippians 1:6); 'the day of the
Lord' (1 Thessalonians 5:2). But there were times when there
was no need to spell it out; everyone knew what day he was
talking about. There was a universal consensus in the Christian
community that this Day was coming. It is an omega point
towards which all history is moving.

In the Old Testament the prophets looked forward to it:

The LORD Almighty has a day in store for all the proud and lofty'
(Isaiah 2:12).

But that day belongs to the LORD, the LORD Almighty - a day of
vengeance, for vengeance on his foes (Jeremiah 46:10).

The day is here! It has come! (Ezekiel 7:10).

The LORD thunders at the head of his army; his forces are beyond
number, and mighty are those who obey his command. The day
of the LORD is great; it is dreadful. Who can endure it? (Joel 2:11).

And so in the New Testament we find the same thing in the words of Jesus,

> Many will say to me on that day, "Lord, Lord did we not prophesy in your name, and in your name drive out demons and perform many miracles?" (Matthew 7:22).

He did not bother to say what he meant by it. He did not need to explain it.

In Acts 17:30-31, Paul the apostle preaches:

> In the past God overlooked such ignorance, but now he commands all people everywhere to repent. For he has set a day when he will judge the world with justice by the man he has appointed. He has given proof of this to all men by raising him from the dead.

And so in 2 Peter 3:10-12, the writer puts it like this:

> But the day of the Lord will come like a thief. The heavens will disappear with a roar; the elements will be destroyed by fire, and the earth and everything in it will be laid bare. Since everything will be destroyed in this way, what kind of people ought you to be? You ought to live holy and godly lives as you look forward to the day of God and speed its coming. That day will bring about the destruction of the heavens by fire and the elements will melt in the heat.

Man has had his day

It will be God's day for man has had his day. For thousands of years man has shaken his fist at God, argued with him, argued about him, hated him, let all the poison come out about how he feels about God. Man has had his day.

Satan too has had his day. He has deceived the nations. All the evil that is in the world can be traced to man and his sin;

sin can be traced to what Satan did by revolting in the heaven of heavens.

In the meantime, God has spoken,

In the past God spoke to our forefathers through the prophets at many times and in various ways, but in these last days he has spoken to us by his Son (Hebrews 1:1-2).

God has given us his Word, but he has never totally, outwardly vindicated himself. He *has* vindicated righteousness at times. He has given a taste of it to the faithful, now and then. But as for God explaining himself, he has never done it.

There are those who say God has a lot to answer for. Yet God has kept quiet. You have heard people curse God and you have heard people say, 'If there is a God, why did he let this happen?' And God kept quiet. Maybe you wonder how could God sit still and let people talk about him like that? But man has had his day, Satan has had his day and one day it will be God's Day. He has promised to speak then, and to explain things.

The Bible calls it 'that Day'. It will be a linear Day; a Day in history that has not come yet. It will be a long Day, how long only God knows. And it will be the last Day; the Day that ends time as we now know it. Jesus said in John 12:48: 'There is a judge for the one who rejects me and does not accept my words; that very word which I spoke will condemn him at the last day.' John on the Isle of Patmos, revealed that Jesus said to him, 'Do not be afraid. I am the First and the Last' (Revelation 1:17). It will be the last Day.

Two phases
This is what Paul means in our text when he refers to the Day: 'His work will be shown for what it is, because the Day will

bring it to light'. Paul does not give the eschatological details here that we may wish for. His intent, in this letter, is simply to show, in part, what will happen then; namely, that the Christian will have a judgment. The judgment will basically be in two phases: phase one will begin at the house of God; phase 2 will take place when the sinner and the ungodly will be judged. If the righteous will scarcely be saved, where will the sinner and the ungodly appear?

The Christian's judgment
What Paul is talking about here is the judgment that will be upon the Christian. As he wrote elsewhere,

> For we must all appear before the judgment seat of Christ, that each one may receive what is due to him for the things done while in the body, whether good or bad (2 Corinthians 5:10).

Even though we are saved, even though we will not go to hell, even though we are renewed in the image of God, even though our bodies have become the temple of the Holy Spirit, we are going to have to give an account of how we have lived as Christians, whether it be good or whether it be bad. And so, though assured of heaven, the Christian will be judged.

What Paul wants us to know here is this: it is going to be God's Day. Until then we may wish to argue with God, but on that Day we will lower our voices. Until then we may wish to argue with each other about God as to who has got it right, while the jury is out, as it were, but on that Day we will stop talking, we will listen, we will watch. There will be no speculative arguing then for the righteous Judge will have his day in court.

There are three things that I want us to see about God's Day.

A Day of truth
The first is that it will be a Day of truth. On that day, God will vindicate himself as being just and righteous.

(i) The truth about the Bible
All that he has said about himself in the Bible will be out in the open. An important aspect of that Day, God's Day, is that it will be a vindication of the Bible. What God has said about himself in the Bible, about creation, about history, and about the fall of Man in the garden of Eden, which was a place on the map, a date in history, will be seen to be true.

(ii) The truth about God's reasons
There will be a vindication of God's reason for permitting evil. That is the question nobody can answer. If we knew the answer to the question, 'Why does God allow suffering?' then we would not need faith. There are those who say, 'Well, explain that one, then I will believe.' Of course they would. Faith is faith when you believe without knowing why God allows evil. If you have to know why God allows evil, then you have said, 'I'm not going to believe until I get that answer.' That question will be answered and when it is answered, you will not need faith; it will be too late. You will be eternally damned.

Faith to be faith is when you vindicate God now. He has said he is righteous, he is just, and you vindicate him now by believing in him. Everybody will vindicate him then, on God's Day. The difference between the Christian and the non-Christian is that the Christian vindicates God in *advance* of that Day; everyone else will have to do it then. And so, God, on that Day, will clear his name, and do it perfectly. Every question long posed by clever and wicked men will be answered.

(iii) The truth about Jesus Christ

All that the scriptures have said about Jesus Christ will be out in the open. The God-Man, the Redeemer, the Saviour will be manifested. 'They will look on me, the one they have pierced', says Zechariah in chapter 12:10. All mankind will see the scars in his hands: 'Look, he is coming with the clouds, and every eye will see him, even those who pierced him' (Revelation 1:7). It will be a vindication of the person of Jesus Christ the Son of God. The only way to be saved will be totally vindicated. Muslims, Buddhists, pagans, Jehovah's Witnesses, world dictators and evil men will bow and confess that Jesus Christ is Lord to the glory of God the Father. They will not be saved, but they will confess, as the apostle Paul says, '... every knee should bow, in heaven and on earth and under the earth, and every tongue confess that Jesus Christ is Lord, to the glory of God the Father' (Philippians 2:10,11).

Three discoveries

On that day of truth, we will discover three things.

Firstly, *who is saved and who is not*. That will include those who are true ministers of the gospel and those who are phonies. On that day we will find out who are saved and who are professing hypocrites. There will be multitudes, untold tens of thousands of church members who will perish and be damned with those who did not even profess to be Christians.

Secondly, on that day of truth, we will discover *what is truth and what is not*. All theological speculations will be exposed for what they are. Theologians like myself will stop talking and we will listen.

Thirdly, on that day of truth we will discover *who walked in the light and who did not*. Paul says, 'His work will be shown for what it is, because the Day will bring it to light. It will be revealed with fire and the fire will test the quality of each man's work'.

Those who walked in the light, according to Paul, receive a reward: 'If what he has built survives, he will receive his reward.' Those who did not walk in the light, though they were saved, will suffer loss: 'If it is burned up, he will suffer loss; he himself will be saved, but only as one escaping through the flames.'

Vindication Day
On that day there will be *three levels of vindication*: first, God will vindicate himself in the light of his glorious power. Second, God will vindicate his Word in the light of its glorious purity. Third, God will vindicate his own, in the light of their motives. Chapter 4:5 says: '...judge nothing before the appointed time'; far better that we lower our voices now, and wait till the Lord comes. He will 'bring to light what is hidden in darkness and will expose the motives of men's hearts'.

You *may* enjoy seeing yourself vindicated; you may find instead that you will watch that *other* person vindicated. For the righteous Judge will decide that. You feel you have been hurt, you feel you have been lied about, someone has walked over you, and you said, 'I just look forward to that Day.' That Day will come. We will find out then whether you and I have vindication coming because, if we have got it coming, we will get it. And God will want you to have it. Nothing will be hidden then, truth will be out.

This is why Paul says in 1 Corinthians 11:31, 'But if we judged ourselves, we would not come under judgment'. That means we must deal squarely with things now; in some cases, we must make restitution now. If I know that anyone has something against me, I will go to him now; I will do everything I can to clear it up. I will be sure there is nothing between me and anybody. You must do so even if you think, 'Oh, I couldn't face so-and-so.' Painful though it would be, far better now than then. It will be too late then on the Day of truth.

A Day of transparency

In Isaiah 29:15 the prophet described those who were so sure that no matter what they did, they would get away with it. It reads like this: 'Woe to those who go to great depths to hide their plans from the LORD, who do their work in darkness and think, "Who sees us? Who will know?" ' As Paul puts it in 1 Corinthian 3:13, '... his work will be shown for what it is'. The Greek word for 'work' is *ergon*.

In Ephesians 2:8-9 we are told we are not saved by works, we are saved by grace through faith. 'Not by works, so that no-one can boast', but Paul went on to write Ephesians 2:10 and a lot of us do not like this verse where he refers to Christians as 'God's workmanship'. There the Greek word is *poema*, and it refers to the mystery of his sovereignty.

This mystery is also referred to in 1 Corinthians 3:9. Paul wrote, 'You are God's building'. There is something very interesting about that word 'building'. It is what God does, and yet it is what we do. It is as though God did it without us, and yet it is as though we did it without him. It is one of those antinomies: twin truths that seem irreconcilable but true. The word for building is used by the apostle eighteen times and is often translated 'edification'. It is as though we are building up ourselves, being edified. Examples of it are found throughout the New Testament:

> Let us therefore make every effort to do what leads to peace and to mutual *edification* (Romans 14:19).

Also in Romans 15:2:

> Each of us should please his neighbour for his good, to *build* him up.

And again in Ephesians 4:12:

... to prepare God's people for works of service, so that the
body of Christ may be *built up* (Ephesians 4:12).

Now what is my point here? On that Day of transparency,
every man's work will be made clear. How much we were built
up, how much we were edified, will be clear. The superstructure will tell it. Some people tell me that they enjoyed a sermon
I have preached, but I'll find out then whether they were trying
to butter me up, to make me feel good, or whether they really
meant it. Whether they meant it will be proved not by their
words, but whether it changed their lives.

It is not just the Christian's work that will be revealed: the
works of all men will be revealed. This needs to be said for in
1 Corinthians 3:13 Paul is simply showing one phase of that
judgment. Turn to Revelation 20:11 where John says,

> Then I saw a great white throne and him who was seated on
> it. Earth and sky fled from his presence, and there was no
> place for them. And I saw the dead, great and small, standing
> before the throne, and books were opened. Another book was
> opened, which is the book of life. The dead were judged
> according to what they had done as recorded in the books.

A lot of people will say, 'I thought you got to heaven by good
works because it says, "They will be judged according to their
works".' All *will be* judged according to their works. God is
going to assess it all. It will be his Day. But John also says, 'If
anyone's name was not found written in the book of life, he
was thrown into the lake of fire' (Revelation 20:15). The way
people know their names are in that book of life is not by
trusting their works, but by transferring all their trust to what
Jesus did on the cross. The way to heaven is by the blood that
he shed.

Revelation by fire

But how will the works of Christians be revealed? God's Day will be revealed with fire.

> ... his work will be shown for what it is, because the Day will bring it to light. It will be revealed with fire, and the fire will test the quality of each man's work (1 Corinthians 3:13).

We must be clear here what Paul is talking about. It is not the work that will be revealed, but the Day. Otherwise the next clause would be redundant because it says, 'the fire will test the quality of each man's work'. It will be the Day that will be revealed by fire.

Verse 13 is in two parts: our work and God's Day. Two things are said of our works: they will be shown for what they are and they will be tested. And what is said of God's Day: it will bring things to light because it will be revealed with fire. God's Day will be a Day of transparency. As Jesus put it, 'So do not be afraid of them. There is nothing concealed that will not be disclosed, or hidden that will not be made known' (Matthew 10:26).

On that Day we will all take off our masks. We all wear them, because we do not want others to know us. We are afraid that we will not be liked if we are really known, so we wear masks to keep from getting hurt. But on that Day, a Day of transparency, the mask will be taken off and we will be known. Others may not like what they see, but we will not have any control over that. Nobody will be pretentious then; nobody will be smug then. Nobody will be self-righteous then. God will say, 'Mask please, R T, give it over.' I will have to take it off. My work will be made manifest, laid bare.

On that Day we will see who really *suffered*. I refer to Revelation 6:10:

They called out in a loud voice, "How long, Sovereign Lord,
holy and true, until you judge the inhabitants of the earth and
avenge our blood?"

On that Day, God is going to enjoy vindicating those who
suffered. God loves to vindicate. And he is going to enjoy
letting everybody see how much you really suffered: you who
dignified the trial and kept quiet about it; you who turned the
other cheek and said nothing. If you talk about it now, you will
get your reward now. But those who were lied about but kept
quiet about it, those who resisted temptation but refused to feel
self-righteous about it, those who sacrificed and got involved
but refused to demand attention, God is going to enjoy
vindicating. It will be God's Day.

The psalmist in Psalm 94:6 says, 'They slay the widow and
the alien; they murder the fatherless. They say, "The LORD does
not see; the God of Jacob pays no heed." ' God will say on that
Day, 'Really? I saw you when you were hurt; I noticed when
you were in pain. I want you to see that I was glorified in your
trial.'

A Day of testing

The third feature about that day will be that *it is a day of testing*.
The last part of our text says, 'It will be revealed with fire, and
the fire will *test* the quality of each man's work'.

The fire will test three things: first, what is *lacking*, namely,
the obedience that erects the superstructure of gold, silver and
precious stones. All will know by the superstructure how
obedient the Christian was.

It will also show what was *lost*, namely, what comes as the
result of intemperate talk and inconsistent traits that erect a
superstructure of wood, hay, straw. For the fire will test our
claims, our character and our conduct.

The fire will test what *lasts*, whether any superstructure is left at all. You may recall when we dealt with the words, gold, silver and precious stones and one of the reasons for their worth was their enduring qualities compared with the combustible materials of wood, hay and straw. What survives the fire will determine whether there is a reward.

You may say, 'I don't care about a reward. What matters is that I am saved.' Well, I can appreciate that. Saved by fire is better than going to hell-fire. But if you are one of those who says, 'I don't need to know about reward,' let me say this: You are building a superstructure whether you like it or not. But with that kind of thinking, are you building a superstructure of gold, silver, precious stones, or wood, hay, straw? It is not a question of whether you believe Paul. You are building a superstructure, and that Day, God's Day, will show the kind of superstructure you chose to build. 'I don't care about reward,' you say. Well, reward mattered to Paul, a rather godly man, I should think! And it mattered to Paul because it mattered to God. That is why Paul could say,

> Do you not know that in a race all the runners run, but only one gets the prize? Run in such a way as to get the prize. Everyone who competes in the games goes into strict training. They do it to get a crown that will not last; but we do it to get a crown that will last forever. Therefore I do not run like a man running aimlessly; I do not fight like a man beating the air. No, I beat my body and make it my slave so that after I have preached to others, I myself will not be disqualified for the prize (1 Corinthians 9:24-27).

The reason for this teaching is so that you can anticipate that on God's Day everything will be laid bare, *except* that which is under the blood of Christ. So that if there are those things in your life that are wrong, but you have repented of them, then 'as far as the east is from the west, so far are our transgressions removed from us'.

Christians need this teaching of the foundation and the superstructure because they need to get on with each other, and if there are those who are not speaking to one another, they need to get it right now. For there can be a superstructure that God can honour and where the ungrieved Spirit of God may settle upon Christians. Then they may know blessing and peace because they have honoured him. Good works matter to God, which is obvious in his Word and it will be seen how much they matter on God's Day. These are not works that are done in order to be saved, but in order to show thanks to God for salvation. And God honours gratitude; he hates ingratitude.

Are you ready for that Day? If you are walking in the light, you will want God's Day to be revealed today. Jesus said, 'So you also must be ready, because the Son of Man will come at an hour when you do not expect him' (Matthew 24:44). Do you want him to come today?

9

The Fiery Trial

> ... the fire will test the quality of each man's work
> (1 Corinthians 3:13).

In this chapter I want to deal mainly with these words in the latter part of 1 Corinthians 3:13.

Fire

If we are to consider how fire tests the quality of each person's work, we must examine what it is that fire does. Essentially, it does two things: it provides light and it gives heat. That is implied in this verse, and that is what is meant when we are told that the fire shall test the quality of every man's work.

(i) Light

Paul informs his readers in verse 13 that God's Day will be 'revealed with fire' and what that means, in part, is that there will be radiant light on that Day, as light is what makes daytime day as opposed to the darkness of night. So on that Day of days, when Jesus Christ comes for the second time, he will come, according to 2 Thessalonians 1:7, 'in blazing fire', and that last Day will be one vast, indescribable ray of light, light so vast that there will be no shadows.

All light in this world gives shadow. I can put my finger on the pulpit and see a shadow coming from where lights are reflected. But on that Day, it will be total, vast, infinite light;

the light of God himself. There will be no shadows and no escaping. Everybody will see clearly; nothing will be hidden, and the quality of each believer's superstructure will be obvious.

(ii) Heat

What about heat? Well, the fire shall test the quality of every man's work, so, Paul continues, 'If what he has built survives, he will receive his reward. If it is burned up, he will suffer loss; he himself will be saved, but only as one escaping through the flames'. The heat will be so intense that only gold, silver, precious stones will survive. Hence the heat will test the quality of every man's work. The superstructure erected with wood, hay, straw, will be burned up.

Work

There is another important word in this phrase: it is the word 'work'. You cannot afford to overlook it. Notice how it is put: the fire will test the quality of each man's 'work'. Paul did not say 'works'. It is quality not quantity that will matter on that Day.

No boasting

At this juncture it is worth remembering that we are talking about what happens to the person already converted. If you are not saved, there is a sense in which this chapter does not apply to you, although God may use it in your life. But the important clarification is this: the work that will be tested is the sum total of our spiritual progress: it is the superstructure, not the foundation. The foundation is what saves, and in verse 11 that we discussed earlier, Paul says, 'For no one can lay any foundation other than the one already laid, which is Jesus Christ'. So the foundation is what saves, and that is not based upon works as Paul wrote in Ephesians 2:8-9: 'For it is by grace you have been saved, through faith - this not from yourselves, it is the gift of God - not by works, so that no-one can boast.'

Loss and gain
The bottom line is this: the foundation is what makes the difference between Heaven and Hell. The superstructure is what makes the difference between reward and loss. It is possible to be saved and suffer loss of reward. As Paul says in verse 15: 'If it is burned up, he will suffer loss; he himself will be saved...'

Fiery trials
Fire therefore is the refiner of the work.

> The trial of your faith being much more precious than of gold that perisheth though it be tried with fire, might be found under praise and honour and glory at the appearing of Jesus Christ (1 Peter 1:7).

We sing of this in the hymn:

> When through fiery trials
>   Thy pathway shall lie,
> My grace, all sufficient
>   Shall be thy supply.
> The flame shall not hurt thee,
>   I only design,
> Thy dross to consume,
>   And thy gold to refine.

The 'fiery trials' test the quality of our work, so that in advance of that Day, they provide a preview of what will happen then.

What does Paul mean by 'work'? It is the sum total of our spiritual progress. We use the expression, 'That's a good piece of work'. When we ask someone, 'Would you do this for me?' and they take several days, and the sum total of their progress we refer to as a 'good piece of work'. It is the sum total of all that preceded. And that is what Paul means by 'work'.

The fiery trial here below prepares us for that ultimate test which we will all experience on the Day of days, which Peter, interestingly, calls the 'Day of Visitation' (1 Peter 2:12 AV). So the fiery trial below gives in advance, as it were, a kind of preview of what will happen on the last Day. What we experience in trials now give us an inkling of what the testing by fire will be like on that Day. I don't know whether you have ever looked at 'trial' like that before? You may never regard 'trial' in the same way again. These words I wish I had read thirty years ago.

The fiery trial below
Everybody is either in a trial now, or between trials. You have either just had one or you are going to have one, or you are having one. But why call it a 'fiery' trial as Peter does? This is because by its light the fire reveals precisely where we are spiritually.

It is apparent of course, that this only appeals to those who have a desire to be godly.

For example, our endurance can be tested during a trial by how we respond to it. If we begin complaining and murmuring, we will acknowledge days (or perhaps even seconds) later that we did not stand up to the trial very well for we did not display a godly nature. Thus trials will test our ability to manifest all the fruits of the Spirit through the heat of trial - love, joy, peace, patience, kindness, goodness, faithfulness, gentleness and self control. They test our work whether we have been walking in the light, and expose how spiritual we really are, which is a sum total of all that has gone on before.

In Deuteronomy 8:2, we read these words:

Remember how the LORD your God led you all the way in the
desert these forty years, to humble you and to test you, in
order to know what was in your heart, whether or not you
would keep his commands.

Again in 2 Chronicles 32:31, it says of Hezekiah, '... God left
him to test him and to know everything that was in his heart'.

What makes a trial, a trial, is that God, as it were, leaves us,
and we feel deserted and betrayed. We say, 'God, I don't
believe this; why would you do this to me? Why desert me at
a moment when I needed you the most?' Is that not the way you
have felt? That's why it is called a 'fiery' trial; God leaves you
to test you, to see what is there. And so, this is the thing about
the trial by fire, it exposes how spiritual we really are - which
is the sum total of all our Christian living so far. We are forced
to see ourselves and we can find out how Christ-like we are.

A dry run

It is something like the mock Preliminary exams that we sat at
school. They let us know how we would do in the real thing,
in the final test. That is the way I want you to see any trial. You
find out just how you are doing. You may feel rather good and
say, 'Well, you don't know what I used to be, how I have
changed;' you may feel pretty awful and say, 'I can't believe
I am really like that.'

A second chance

But the good news is that God is still dealing with us, and there
is time, because God will give us a second chance, a second
time around here in this life. That is the big difference between
the fiery trial below and that final Day. Fire by its heat reveals
the quality of our superstructure up to that moment. If we have

built upon the foundation gold, silver and precious stones, then
there is a good possibility we will dignify the trial. But if we
have been in the meantime building upon the foundation
wood, hay and straw, we can predict we will fail the test. We
are made to see how much more spiritual progress is needed
through every trial.

I can recall the day when I had to ask myself, do I believe
what I preach? I was preaching that my response to trial was
reflecting my spirituality as well as being a preview of what
would happen on that Day. Yet I was the world's greatest
murmurer and complainer! I cannot say that I am totally healed
of it but I believe it was the greatest turning-point in my
spiritual life.

When James wrote, 'Consider it pure joy, my brothers,
whenever you face trials of many kinds (1:2), he did so because
we do not really know how spiritual we are until we undergo
a trial. And we will know how we stand for a trial below does
two things: first, it shows us where we actually are in our walk
with Christ; secondly, it shows us what is needed to pass the
test the second time around. If we fail a driving test, for
example, we are always told why we failed. Do you remember
when you had to take your driving test? The hardest thing in
the world that I have ever had to pass in my life was the British
driving test! My viva at Oxford for my DPhil was like eating
strawberries and cream compared to passing the driving test!
I will not say how many times I had to sit it!

Tests of the trial

(i) Truth
Now in the fiery trial below, there are four things that are
tested: the first is the truth of what you believe.

There is nothing like a fiery trial to test the validity of what you believe. Bad theology will not fare well in the fiery trial, so doctrine is very important. A fiery trial proves that if your theology does not help you in the time of trial, it is not worth anything.

(ii) Speech

The second thing to be tested in the fiery trial is our speech. How well you have controlled your tongue is exposed in the trial and sometimes, I fear many times, intemperate speech exasperates or even initiates the very trial that you are in. God allowed it to happen so that you might be exposed. Sometimes you are in a trial, therefore, because you are the one that brought it on.

But a tongue that has been controlled brings a great sense of divine approval under fire. This is why Peter wrote:

> But in your hearts set apart Christ as Lord. Always be ready to give an answer to everyone that asks you to give the reason for the hope that you have. But do this with gentleness and respect, keeping a clear conscious, so that those who speak maliciously against your good behaviour in Christ may be ashamed of their slander (1 Peter 3:15-16).

When the Day of the Lord comes it will be wonderful to note your progress or embarrassing to see your failure. Nevertheless, if you fail here and now, wait for the second time around. You may well get another chance; pray that you will.

(iii) Strength of character

The third thing tested is strength of character. The fiery trials here below will show whether solid Christian character has been in the making. Proverbs 24:10 says, 'If thou faint in the day of adversity, thy strength is small' (AV). We tell what we

are under fire. If we have been building the superstructure of
gold, silver and precious stones, then there will be a manifes-
tation of love, joy, peace and longsuffering. But if we have
been building a superstructure of wood, hay and straw, then in
the time of trial you know what will come out - jealousy, rage,
vengeance, and you will not have any peace at all. Remember,
the key to strength of character is the tongue. Then if you feel
exposed and feel awful, pray God you will get a second chance.

(iv) Trust
The fourth thing to be tested is your trust. What I mean by that
is this: when the trial comes, do you remain calm? Do you have
a calm trust in God? Or do panic and unbelief set in? Are you
bowled over by the sudden trial, or is there calm? And can you
say and really mean, without a whimper, 'The Lord gives, the
Lord takes away, blessed be his name'. The aim of the superstructure of gold, silver and precious stones, is solid and simple
trust in God. And at the end of the day, that is what is tested,
whether in the heat of the moment your trust is unwavering.

Prepare yourself
How then do we prepare for the fiery trial? If you are in the 'in-
between time', as Richard Bewes puts it, how do you prepare?
Perhaps you are in it right now, how do you prepare for the trial
which will surely come?

There are three stages that lie behind the principle that we
dealt with previously - the principle being 1 Corinthians 11:31:
'But if we judged ourselves, we would not come under
judgment'. Although it is a verse Paul uses in the context of
taking the Lord's Supper, it is a very important verse for the
whole of Christian living.

Guarantees for failure

Three things lie behind that verse, or to put it another way: what is the sure guarantee of wood, hay, straw?

(i) Undiscovered sin

God never brings to your mind sin that you are already convicted of and have repented of. In other words, he only focuses on sin that has not been brought to your attention. It has always been there but for some reason you did not realise it.

For years I did not see it, but I was such a murmurer and such a complainer. I am sure everyone else who knew me saw it because others always see our faults! We just cannot see them in ourselves. But there came a time, when, thank God, he just grabbed me and showed me. I had to see that I was responsible for everything I did through those years, and if God had taken me home, I would have been saved by fire. I was not building a superstructure of gold, silver and precious stones - of this I am sure. In this respect I was not learning how to dignify the trial.

But why was I not aware of that sin before? The simple answer is that I was not listening to God. I was not spiritual enough to recognise it. It is no coincidence that great spirituality always carries with it a great sense of sin. Have you ever wondered why it is the greatest saints have always seen themselves as the greatest sinners? They just get so close to God that they see sin in themselves that other people cannot see because they are not so near. Isaiah saw the radiant glory of God and cried out, 'Woe is me!' (Isaiah 6:1-8).

When God does expose your sin to you I can understand if you say, 'Lord, why didn't you tell me that before?' But it is because you were not listening. It is crucial therefore to hear his voice, for it is an encouraging thing that God stays with you and you *can* be renewed again unto repentance.

(ii) Unconfessed sin

Why does anybody confess sin? It is because we are ashamed. We can confess sin because we are truly sorry, and when we are sorry we turn from it. That does not mean we will be perfect, but we will loathe ourselves for our imperfection and try by the grace of God, not to repeat it, with the tongue, with impatience, with panic. And so, if God puts his finger on your sin, but you do not confess it, you will build a superstructure of wood, hay and straw. The moment you see the sin but decide to cling to it, you guarantee that you will fail in the trial.

(iii) Unrestituted sin

The logical step from this is the third point which means putting things right with another person. That's what to restitute means, to put something right. Unrestituted sin is when you refuse to make things right. So why would you make restitution? There are two simple reasons to do so. First, you will give another person peace. Paul said in Romans 14:19, 'Do the things that make for peace, whereby you may edify one another' (AV). The second reason is that you will get peace yourself by doing it.

Not all confessed sin requires this, of course. This could be only an occasional occurrence, but there comes a time when you have no choice but to put it right with a fellow-Christian. You may say, 'Well, when will I know to do that?' It is when you know that they know you have hurt them. And when you make restitution they will be so glad! It will give them peace; you will feel so good because you will be at peace.

However, if you have wronged a person and they do not know it, then keep quiet about it. If you tell them they will be hurt unnecessarily. Leave it alone!

Building a superstructure of wood, hay and straw therefore shows how to do the reverse - we do not have any difficulty then seeing how to build a superstructure of gold, silver and precious stones. First, it is when sin is discovered and we rejoice when this happens. Second, when we confess it, and third, if necessary, we put it right. Those are the three stages that lie behind 1 Corinthians 11:32. In other words, deal with it now, and it will not show up then. Sweep it under the carpet now, and it will come out then.

The fiery trial above

The main thing that Paul is after when he says, 'The fire shall test the quality of each man's work' is, of course, what of the fiery trial *above*. This refers to the sum total of the Christian's spiritual progress at the time of the second coming of Jesus.

Spiritual progress can be defined as the degree to which one has walked in the light, the degree to which one has dealt with sin in one's life. What will be revealed will be whether we are in a state of being renewed to repentance, and whether God is still dealing with us. And all this comes down to one thing: whether we have responded to chastening, either internal chastening, when God deals inwardly through the Word, or external chastening when he has to do something pretty drastic to get our attention.

The one whose superstructure is of wood, hay and straw will be exposed by his inability to be renewed unto repentance and by his failure to respond to chastening. That is why we read in Hebrews 6:8:

> But land that produces thorns and thistles is worthless and is in danger of being cursed. In the end it will be burned.

These echo the words of Jesus in John 15:6:

> If any one does not remain in me, he is like a branch that is

thrown away and withers; such branches are picked up, thrown into the fire and burned.

Similarly, 1 Corinthians 3:14-15:

If what he has built survives, he will receive his reward. If it is burned up, he will suffer loss; he himself will be saved, but only as one escaping through the flames.

Similarities

Are the fiery trail below and the fiery trial above alike? To recall our previous illustration, in what way would a mock exam (a trial here below) and the real thing (the trial above) be alike? First, they are both unexpected; they come without warning. Second, both expose where we are in our spiritual progress. Third, both will be a time of pressure and testing, and fourth, they come from God.

Differences

But what are the differences between the fiery trial below and that one which is coming, when the Day will be revealed by fire?

First, the trial below may be hidden from others. You can be in a trial and nobody know it, but God's fire on that Day of days will bring us out into the open.

The second difference: the trial below is usually brought on by earthly pressures - people or perhaps our own stupidity. It may be persecution, it may be financial difficulty. But on that day the fire will be God's fire, without the need of earthly pressures to show where we are.

The third difference: the trial below sometimes comes by way of a Satanic attack. If you are in a fiery trial now, the devil is not far away. The fiery trial may be the devil attacking you, but on the Day of the Second Coming it will be entirely the intervention of God sending his Son with fire and glory. The devil will have no part in that trial.

The fourth difference, and perhaps the ultimate point which needs to be made, is that the trial below exposes where we are in our progress, but there's hope that when you fail, God will come a second time around and you will do better. But on that Day, it is final; there will be no repeats, that is it.

Do you see why James said, 'Consider it pure joy, my brothers, whenever you face trials of many kinds' (1:2)? It lets us know how we are doing. It is preparation for the Day of days; it shows where we are spiritually and it is showing that God is still working to get our attention. For there is coming a Day when there will be no warning; there will be no second examination. Our work will be tested. It will be the sum total of all our spiritual progress; we will have our final exam. No repeats or resits and we will live throughout eternity with no opportunity to build up treasure in heaven. But you can do that now.

I do not know who said it but it has been quoted all over the world many times:

> Only one life,
>   'Twill soon be passed,
> Only what's done
>   For Christ will last.

10

Pure Gold

If what he has built survives, he will receive his reward.
(1 Corinthians 3:14)

In this verse the apostle Paul elaborates on three things that he has already stated: reward, superstructure and how much of the superstructure remains after the fire of the final Day.

The concept of reward he raised first in verse 8 when he wrote, 'The man who plants and the one who waters have one purpose, and each will be rewarded according to his labour'. Now he is beginning to unfold when that reward will be received.

The superstructure is something that is implied in verse 11, when he says, 'For no-one can lay any foundation other than the one already laid, which is Jesus Christ'. But how much of that superstructure will remain after the fire is seen in verse 13: '... his work will be shown for what it is, because the Day will bring it to light. It will be revealed with fire, and the fire will test the quality of each man's work'.

Survive/Remain

Now the word, 'survive' comes from the Greek word, *meno*, and it gives us the English word 'remain'. In fact, the NIV uses that word, 'remain', in its translation of John 15. From John's first letter we know that this word is a favourite word of John's where it appears often. Perhaps its best known use is, however, in John 15:4: '*Abide* in me and I in you', which the NIV translates as '*Remain* in me and I will remain in you'. It is a similar meaning in 1 Corinthians 3:14 where the NIV translates the word as 'survive'.

Now the fact that we are all going to stand before God and give an account, even though we are not going to go to Hell, is an awesome thing. And when you think about this, the possibility that you and I could build upon the foundation a superstructure so solid, substantial and survivable that even the intense heat that accompanies the Second Coming of Jesus does not destroy, it can do two things: it can make you feel thankful in anticipation of that Day, and it can make you feel unworthy.

But this is the kind of teaching that I would have thought should be applicable to anybody no matter how insignificant you feel. God is no respecter of persons, and you may feel that you do not matter, but I want you to know that you will be judged just like anybody else. Whether you come from aristocracy, or if you are a member of the Royal Family, you will only be saved or lost by whether or not your trust is in Christ alone. And if you are saved, your superstructure will be based upon the quality of your life and walking in the light, and will have nothing whatever to do with your profile here below.

Barak

So any one of us could build a lasting superstructure. The thing I want to underline is that the weakest Christian can still do it. You may say, 'Well now, look here, I am not able to do this or that, and I just feel I must be the weakest Christian that ever lived'. It is worth remembering the Old Testament character, Barak. Barak was the equivalent of an Israeli general in the day of the Judges. Deborah, a judge in Israel during that period, was told by the Lord that the time had come to defeat the enemy. So she turned to Barak and said, 'Take ten thousand of your men and meet on Mount Nebo and the Lord is going to deliver the enemy into your hand.' Barak said, 'No, I just do not think I want to do that. I'm not ready.' But he said, 'Deborah, if you'll go with me, I'll go.' She says, 'Well, now, just a minute, if I go, you are not going to get any glory, it will go to a woman.' He said, 'It's all right.'

Now why did Barak do that? He did that because he wanted to see Israel win but he was afraid they would not win by himself, and he asked for Deborah to go with him. And a woman, Jael, in fact, got the glory, and we have the Song of Deborah in Judges 5:24; it is not about Barak. He felt like he was a nobody, nevertheless in Hebrews 11, when the writer comes down through the Old Testament, who does he choose to mention as having faith? Barak. And I find that so encouraging; that the weakest Christian can do it. The reason Barak was given that glory was that he did not want the glory then. That is just the tip of the iceberg on the way reward will be given on that Day of days.

After the fire
A superstructure of pure gold may be an unattainable target when we consider that the *perfect* reward would require a perfect life. I do not know even what that superstructure of pure gold may be - I am out of my depth in this regard. Yet it would be helpful to gather some ideas as to that reward. I believe there are four components in this superstructure of pure gold and in examining them we can discover how this superstructure may be erected.

Persevering in grace
In 1 Corinthians 5 we find Paul dealing with one who was not persevering in grace. He was indulging in the kind of sin that

was a disgrace to the church - even Gentiles would not get involved in it. Paul wrote, '... hand this man over to Satan so that the sinful nature may be destroyed and his spirit saved on the day of the Lord'. He was not persevering. Some Christians will be found, I believe, in a backslidden state - to some degree - at the time of the Second Coming of Jesus. I want to ask you a question: can you recall a time in your own life, when if the Lord had come then, you would be very ashamed indeed? You did not have what John called 'boldness in the day of judgment', far from it. You knew that you were living in fear; you knew things were not right. That is not the way to receive reward. We must do the opposite: persevere in grace. But how do we do it? It means three things.

(i) Abiding in faith

This is having faith in Christ's sacrifice, in his substitutionary work, in his satisfaction. It means being found 'relying on his love' as John put it in 1 John 4:16. This is what saves us from self-righteousness at the time of the Second Coming of Jesus as well as saving us from self-righteousness now. And if we think it through, and see the implications that come from relying on his love, then we will be convicted of being self-righteous and judgmental, I promise you.

(ii) Abiding in faithfulness

We must also abide in faithfulness. In chapter 4:2, Paul writes, 'Now it is required that those who have been given a trust must prove faithful'. Also, Jesus said to the bishop of the Church of Smyrna, 'Be faithful, even to the point of death and I will give you the crown of life' (Revelation 2:10). It is not enough that you once made a definite commitment. The question is: will you be found committed when Jesus comes?

(iii) Abiding with the fruit

Persevering in grace means producing fruit that is implied not only in 1 Corinthians 3 but in the words of Jesus in John 15:2: 'He cuts off every branch in me that bears no fruit', and verse 4: 'Remain in me and I will remain in you. No branch can bear fruit by itself; it must remain in the vine'.

Now Paul could have followed through with an earlier metaphor which comes out in chapter 3:8, when he says that, 'The man who plants and the man who waters have one purpose' and again in verse 9, 'For we are God's fellow-workers, you are God's field'. He could have used the concept, therefore, of vegetation and fruit, but he chose instead to talk about the superstructure: the building.

So that is the first thing. To have a superstructure of pure gold, one must be persevering in grace. Now if one is truly found persevering in grace, I doubt not that he will have all that I am going to be discussing in the next three points. Any one of these four propositions logically followed says everything that the other three say. But the four propositions cohere; they also clarify what it is that will survive the fire: they show what will be rewarded.

Unrewarded obedience

Another way of describing this building block which goes toward erecting the superstructure of pure gold is to think of it as what went unnoticed. This gets to the heart of the matter regarding this question of reward. The rule of thumb here, though there will be an exception and that I shall refer to, is *recognition now, no reward then*. For example, in Matthew 6, Jesus describes the Pharisees who whenever they contributed anything would sound a trumpet and let everybody know they were giving. If they prayed they wanted everybody to know they prayed. If they fasted they would give everybody the impression they fasted. They wanted their righteousness to be seen and Jesus said, 'They *have* their reward, that's it. They wanted to be noticed? They got it.'

If you will insist on people noticing you and praising you and giving you the credit, you may get it, but remember you cannot have it both ways. You make a choice, but if you show contempt for earthly recognition, you are building a super-structure of pure gold. God will see to it that you are remembered at the judgment seat of Christ. The way to build a superstructure of straw therefore is just make sure you get your recognition *now*. You can be unsubtle about it or you can *quietly* pull one or two strings. People do not know that is what you are doing - but God knows.

I once knew a man who was regarded as being very generous because he would give great donations to the church. The difficulty was we all knew about it! He made sure it was known. He could not just put money in the collection plate or bag, he had to hand-deliver it! That way the word leaked out and that was what he wanted. I do not say that the church is not going to profit, but that person will not have a reward from God.

The same thing is true if you sacrifice for God. You make sure somebody finds out how much you have suffered and all you have gone through, and are going through in your struggle. They will notice, but that is it.

Consider the scenario:

(i) Unrecognized results
This is the thing to which unrewarded obedience refers. You got results, nobody noticed. You saw God work through what you did, but you wanted everybody to notice it. God saw it but that was not enough for you; you wanted people to notice it. Well, you either wait for it to come out later, or you give into the temptation which may be very great, not to keep quiet about it.

(ii) Unsought recognition

If we think again about Barak we find that he did not want any glory. He just wanted his people to win the victory. It never crossed his mind that some day, three or four thousand years later, he would be recorded in Hebrews 11 as a hero of faith. If someone went to him in Heaven and said, 'Guess what, Barak, you are regarded as a hero!', he would say, 'You've got to be joking!' But you see, all he wanted was for Israel to win. And that is an encouraging thing; recognition eventually came which was unsought.

If what you did gets noticed but you did not seek it, it is rather different. Sometimes people are going to notice things, but if you are not seeking recognition now, nobody is going to diminish your reward on that Day. And sometimes God does allow some to get recognition below. The question is, did you seek it? Or did God just do it.

Unsought recognition pleases God and he may choose to give you a taste of glory below. But I have got a theory and it is this: high profile below is ominous. The higher your profile the less likely is great reward in heaven, unless you are a very unusual person. This is one of the reasons that James said, 'Not many of you should presume to be teachers, my brothers, because you know that we who teach will be judged more strictly' (James 3:1).

Some Christians are well known and highly thought of in many places. In some cases God is the only explanation for this, for he has put them in such places of prominence. But it does not follow that they will automatically receive a reward at the judgment seat of Christ. Quite the opposite could be the case. High profile here below will mean nothing in Heaven. I would go so far as to say that high profile here raises the likelihood of our building a superstructure of straw. Why? Because the temptation for even *more* earthly recognition is greater. The person who can resist this temptation is exceeding rare. It will be interesting to see how many famous Christians will actually receive a reward at the judgment seat of Christ.

(iii) Unvindicated righteousness

This third meaning of unrewarded obedience, unvindicated righteousness, occurs when a righteous deed was criticised or misunderstood. Do you know what it is to take your stand in a particular situation and have nobody agree with you? Now it could be you were wrong. You may not know. At the end of the day the righteous Judge will do the vindicating.

However, perhaps you were right. Let us say you have taken your stand because you were honouring God and following the Holy Spirit and there was not a vestige of ego or pride in it. You were just doing it for the honour of God alone and as a result you were lied about, and people believed those lies. You made no attempt to put the record straight. You could have cleared your name but you did not. That is what God likes. Had you cleared your name, you would have built a superstructure of straw, but you kept quiet, and God's heart was moved. Your silence was golden - pure gold in fact. In 2 Thessalonians 1:6, in the very same paragraph when Paul talks about the Second Coming of Jesus in blazing fire, he also said, 'It is a righteous thing with God to recompense tribulation to them that trouble you' (AV).

But we want to know when this will happen. The NIV is very clear: this will happen when Jesus comes in fire, in glory. There is no promise of vindication this side of Heaven. You may get it, but there is no promise of it. Maybe you were tempted to speak out and clear your own name but on that day you will be glad you kept your mouth shut, because God loves to clear the name of those who have been mistreated:

Therefore judge nothing before the appointed time; wait till the Lord comes. He will bring to light what is hidden in darkness and will expose the motives of men's hearts. At that time each will receive his praise from God (1 Corinthians 4:5).

Resilient love

This third building block of the golden superstructure can only be the case when love becomes a habit. There have been those of us who felt we had done something so wonderful because we totally forgave somebody who did something naughty to us. We did it once and we were so proud of it. It was such an unusual thing, you can never forget it! But that is not resilient love; resilient love is when love is not an ordeal but a habit, so that when they lie about you next, you just bounce back and you do not try to clear your name or try to set the record straight. It is when you are not even aware any more that you do it.

(i) The absence of fear

In his first letter, John states a truth about resilient love. He says, 'there is no fear in love' (1 John 4:18). In this instance the NIV translation improves on the Authorised Version for it goes on to say, 'But perfect love drives out fear, because fear has to do with punishment'. It means you want to punish somebody who has hurt you; you want to make them look bad; you want to give them the cold shoulder; you want to tell what they did to you. And do you see why is it that we are afraid? We are insecure.

The best illustration at this point is the story of how Joseph revealed himself to his brothers in Egypt. He spoke to them in private with no-one listening so nobody would know who had hurt him or what had been done to him. He wanted to protect his brothers. This was resilient love. It is when there is such an absence of fear that you do not want anybody to know what they did to you. I want to ask you a question: has somebody hurt you and have you told anybody that they hurt you? Why did you tell them? You wanted to punish the one that hurt you; you wanted to make them look bad. But there is no fear in love.

Another thing about Joseph was that he did not want his brothers to be afraid of him. If you want to keep somebody afraid of you, it is because you are afraid and you are insecure and you want to be able to control them. But fear has no place here. Joseph shows us in practice what resilient love is all about.

(ii) The art of forgetting
In 1 Corinthians 13, the 'Love' chapter of the Bible, Paul says that love 'keeps no record of wrongs'. However, what is the other side of the coin? It also means keeping no record of rights. Why do you need to remember your rights? So that you can call attention to it? It is the same evil when you call attention to someone's wrongs and you keep a record of their wrongs. It is a fact that 90% of marriages that are on the rocks right now could be healed overnight, if they lived by this: the art of forgetting. If you cannot learn it, you will be a builder with straw.

(iii) The accommodation of faults
How great is your ability to embrace people with faults? Instead, do you judge them? Perhaps you say, 'Well, look here, somebody needs to say something to them.' But God dealt with you. If this is your attitude then you are judging. We read, 'Do not judge, or you too will be judged. For in the same way as you judge others, you will be judged ... ' (Matthew 7:1-2). Obviously he has not finished yet with *you*, because you cannot accept people with all those faults! God will deal with that other person sooner, if you leave them alone. God dealt with you and look how long he waited!

Enduring with dignity

Can you think of any moment lately when you were glad Jesus
had not come? If he had come would he have found you
complaining, criticising or ready to give up? Perhaps you have
a handicap or you have a low-paying job. Perhaps you know
what it is to be lonely; perhaps you were passed over; perhaps
you feel that life has passed you by; perhaps you feel it is unfair
that you had to have the lousy wife you have or the lousy
husband you have got, or the illness?

But what is enduring with dignity? It means that at the
Second Coming of Jesus, beware that you are not *questioning*
God. Beware of bitterness against him.

It also means do not be found *quenching*. That is trying to
abort a God-ordained trial. Every trial has a timescale and it
will end. There is no trial given to you that is not common to
man from which God will not make a way of escape. Now that
is the promise of God's Word. It does not matter what the trial
is - you may say, this one is too big for me - it is not. The devil
will make you think it is too big for you and you think at long
last you have found a loophole whereby you can complain.
You try to quench what the Spirit has done by giving you a
trial. It will end but if you try to end it before it is over, you will
build a superstructure of straw.

However tempted you sometimes are to give up, at the
Second Coming of Jesus Christ make sure that you are not
found *quitting*. This, of course, goes back to the very first point
in this chapter: persevering in grace. No matter what, in the
words of Winston Churchill, 'We shall never, never, never
surrender'. The three Hebrews said, 'Our God is able to deliver
us, but if not, we will not bow down' (Daniel 3).

As you read this you may be undergoing a trial greater than
which cannot be conceived, and maybe no-one has a clue what
you are going through, and you are almost ready to quit. *Don't!*

Don't! Your endurance in this trial of your faith will bring praise, honour and glory to Jesus Christ on his appearing. Dignify the trial even though your faith is tried by fire. *Do not* quit! You are the one that has an opportunity to have what Paul calls, 'reward'.

It is necessary, then, for us to consider carefully what our superstructures are made of. What matters is what will survive on that Day - and that Day is coming. It may be soon. Every day in the meantime counts. We are all building a superstructure. It takes nothing to build a superstructure of straw and yet, the superstructure of pure gold is the best way to live.

11

The Approval Of God

If what he has built *survives,* he will receive his reward.
(1 Corinthians 3:14)

We come face to face now with this matter of reward. Other
words for it in the New Testament are 'prize', 'crown', and I
could go on and on with other synonyms. Now I can tell you
exactly what the reward is. The reward is God's saying to us,
'Well done!' That is it. 'Well,' you say, 'is that all there is to
it?' If that disappoints you, I have to tell you that you probably
will not receive a reward in Heaven. The reward goes to those
who want this more than anything in the world - just to hear
God say, 'Well done!' This is why the apostle Paul could say
in 2 Corinthians 5:9, 'We make it our goal to please him.' Did
you ever notice that? We make it our aim to please him.

And what do you suppose is the very next thing that Paul
says after that? Having said we make it our aim to please him
he says, 'For we must all appear before the judgment seat of
Christ, that each one may receive what is due to him for the
things done while in the body, whether good or bad'. Peter
calls this 'a rich welcome' (2 Peter 1:11).

The promise of reward
There are a number of things that I want to extract from this
verse with regard to reward. The first is the promise of reward.
You will notice that the verse at the head of the chapter is a

promise. It is even a calculated promise and certainly no afterthought. It is not something that God suddenly decided to do - 'Well, here's what I'm going to do for those who have sought to please me!' No, it is carefully thought through, and not only that, what God is doing in promising reward, is dignifying his creation of us, the very way he chose to make us.

Have you ever wondered why it is that frail man needs approval? Why do we all want approval? God made us that way and the need for approval is what lies behind God's promise of reward. The one who says, 'I don't care about that sort of thing' either is not being honest and has become very self-righteous, or is so deeply hurt that he or she is no longer in touch with his true feelings.

Now the interesting thing is, the less spiritual we are, the more we need man's approval. The more spiritual we are, the more we want God's approval. God is not against our having recognition by others, as long as we aim to please him first. He is delighted to share us.

The three Rs
Three things make up the reward: ratification, recognition, realisation. Ratification is simply confirming what we were when we were on this earth. Recognition is when God lets all recognise the surviving superstructure after the fire of that Day. Realisation is when each of us knows exactly what God thinks. And so God is not against our having recognition by others as long as we aim to please him first and he gets all the glory. But if we seek recognition from man we will forfeit the ultimate reward of hearing him say, 'Well done!'

We must all appear
If it is a calculated promise, it is also a challenging promise. Think of these words: 'we must all appear'. There will be no

exceptions. It will not be like those who when they travel from country to country are not requested to go through customs. They enter through the diplomatic gate with no checks, no questions asked. Oh no! Paul says we must all appear before the judgment seat of Christ.

It requires maturity. Paul can put it like this in 1 Corinthians 13:11: 'When I was a child, I talked like a child, I thought like a child, I reasoned like a child. When I became a man, I put childish things behind me'. It means we must grow up. All of us are congenitally allergic to this real maturity. We want to stay as we were; we do not want to get old; we do not want to mature; but we will all give an account of things done in the body, whether they be good or bad.

The greatest challenge

It is the greatest challenge there ever was: greater than winning the World Cup; greater than getting the gold at the Olympics; better than getting a First at University. What we are looking at tests the human spirit to the ultimate degree. Then one hopes to hear the Judge of all the earth, say 'Good!' You may face an intellectual challenge but that is nothing because you may survive that challenge due to a great brain. Similarly, a physical challenge is nothing because some have natural athletic ability. But when we must give an account before the judgment seat of Christ - our spiritual challenge - all of us are equal. Not a single person had a head start. We are all sinners and God is no respecter of persons. We have all been saved by grace. It is the greatest challenge that ever was and you may feel that you were pushed behind the door when it came to getting a particular kind of invitation to do this, or that you have not been given a lot of ability, and you have not been noticed. But in God's scheme the most insignificant person can be told by God, 'Well done!' and all the high and the mighty can be ignored.

A conditional promise

Notice how Paul puts it. He says, 'If what he has built *survives,* he will receive his reward.' It is a conditional promise. In other words, the word is not automatic for every Christian. You may have thought that all Christians would get the same reward. Perhaps you say, 'If you are saved, you are saved. We are all going to go to our reward.' Not so. It is those whose workmanship results in a surviving superstructure that will receive it.

The problem of reward

Why do I call the reward a problem? The reason is that some Christians are put off by the very idea of reward. It is almost beneath them.

A very British idea

I was talking to my friend Robert Amess of Duke Street Baptist Church, and he said, 'Remember, when you preach your sermon on reward next Sunday that thinking British Christians are put off by the idea of reward'. Well I know that! I have not lived over here for nearly twenty years for nothing! And I too was once of the opinion, and I held it for years, that being saved is all that matters. I could have defended the idea because I felt that a reward competed with the glory and honour of Christ and his atoning work on the cross. Somehow the idea of a reward sounded cheap and though there is something in the Bible about it, I said, 'Well, we don't need to go into that really, it just appeals to carnally-motivated Christians who are more concerned with reward than going to heaven.'

Sanctification: assurance or reward

Nevertheless I have had to think about this a lot and I think I have given more thought to this than any other subject. It was the heart of my thesis at Oxford; it is what I have concentrated on most. And it comes to this: the place of sanctification in God's plan for us. Sanctification is ultimately one of two things; ultimately you have one of two views. Either you will see sanctification as the ground of your assurance of salvation, that is how you know you are saved. Or, it will be the basis of reward in Heaven. You say, 'Well, there must be another option.'

In truth there is none, if you think it through. Let us examine these two positions further. If your view is that sanctification is the ground of *assurance*, namely the proof that you are saved, then you would say that if a person is not living a godly life, he was never converted. That used to be my opinion. Alternatively, if you say that sanctification is the basis of *reward*, but you still know that you are saved, then obviously you have got your assurance elsewhere rather than by looking at your good works, namely from Christ alone. This is now my belief: I know I am saved solely because Jesus paid my debt. That is how I know I am going to heaven.

The danger with the former stance is that in working to be certain of one's salvation, one competes with the honour and glory of Christ. And I have a horror of anything that smacks of saying, 'Well, make your calling and election sure, and to be sure you are saved ensure those works are there.' That is what competes with the honour and glory of Christ.

Three problems
If you continue with this belief and persist that the way you know you are saved is because you are sufficiently godly, three things follow, I guarantee it. First, you will look, sooner or later, to your good works for your assurance to be firm. Second, if you are very conscientious about it, you will always have some doubt whether you really are saved. Third, you are one step away from salvation by works.

Motivation toward holiness

Well, what is sanctification? It is the inevitable process of
being made holy because you are saved. Sanctification is
inevitable however only by degrees. If all converts automatically manifested perfect obedience, there would be no need for
the New Testament. There would be no need for Paul to write
letters to his converts, as he had to do to the church in Corinth.
The fact is, some Christians grow faster than others; some are
more obedient than others. This is partly why it was God's idea
to bring in eschatology to motivate weak Christians. This is the
way 1 Corinthians 3 began. He says 'you are still worldly', and
one way of stirring them is to say to them 'We must all appear
before the judgment seat of Christ' (2 Corinthians 5:10). This
was used as a way to motivate them towards holiness. Paul says
in the next verse how this affected him: 'Since then we know
what it is to fear the Lord, we try to persuade men.' Elsewhere
he explains his motivation in other terms: 'I beat my body and
make it my slave so that after I have preached to others, I myself
will not be disqualified for the prize' (1 Corinthians 9:27).

The pattern of reward

There is a pattern to this theme of reward as revealed in the
New Testament. The main word for 'reward' which is *misthos*
in Greek, appears twenty-nine times and there are several other
words which have an equivalent meaning, namely, crown,
prize, inheritance, boldness and being unashamed. But I want
to deal with two things. First, how Jesus referred to the idea of
reward or its equivalent, and secondly, how some New
Testament writers referred to reward.

In Matthew 5:11-12 Jesus said,

Blessed are you when people insult you, persecute you an
falsely say all kinds of evil against you because of me. Rejo

and be glad, because great is your reward in heaven, for in the same way they persecuted the prophets who were before you.

In Matthew 5:44 he instructs his disciples to love and pray for their persecutors. Reward comes *to those who pray for those who persecute them*. But perhaps when we pray for those who lie about us, were the Lord to ask, 'What if I really do bless them?' to be honest you might have to reply, 'Well I don't expect you really to bless them, you just told me to say it. You wouldn't really bless them, would you, Lord?' That does not count. But when you really pray for them and can truthfully say, 'God, don't hurt them! Don't let anything happen to them!', reward will be yours. Even as Moses interceded for a generation of Israelites, and said, 'Don't hurt them!' He stood up for them. That is what ensured him of a great reward.

Jesus also linked reward to *building up treasure in heaven*. In Matthew 6:20 we read,

> But store up for yourselves treasures in heaven, where moth and rust do not destroy, and where thieves do not break in and steal. For where your treasure is, there your heart will be also.

Again in Matthew 10:42 we also find the words,

> And if anyone gives even a cup of cold water to one of these little ones because he is my disciple, I tell you the truth, he will certainly not lose his reward.

Thus the *smallest gesture of kindness*, Jesus says, will guarantee reward.

I often use the term, ordinary obedience, to describe Christian living. How do the New Testament writers describe the reward for ordinary obedience?

For Peter, ordinary obedience would result in *a rich welcome* (2 Peter 1:11). James wrote, 'Blessed is the man who endureth temptation. When he is tried he will receive *the crown of life*' (1:12). Paul said *the crown* would be given to all those who love his appearing (2 Timothy 4:8) and John stated, 'Herein is our love made perfect, that we may have *boldness* in the day of judgment' (1 John 4:17).

But once in a while there was something extraordinary. To refer back to a previous point - of praying for those who persecute you - that is something extraordinary. And Jesus said, 'Rejoice and be glad, for great is your reward in heaven'. Again when we give to those who are our enemies and hope for nothing in return, our reward shall be great (Luke 6:35).

I think this is why the apostle Paul, in 1 Corinthians 9, realising that when a person has been converted like he had, struck down on the road to Damascus, after being such a blasphemer, and his conversion is total, he could never do anything to get a reward for it, God had done it all. He had to look pretty hard for any way to earn his reward, and he said, 'I have come up with a way, I will preach the gospel at Corinth and I won't take a penny from them'. Therefore at the end of the chapter he can say, 'I want the prize'. He also adds, 'I keep my body under lest having preached to others, I myself should be rejected for the prize'. He did not want anything to lessen his chance of gaining his reward for his was particularly strenuous to win.

There is also reward to be gained through *unusual suffering endured with dignity.* I could spend a lot of time on this topic but just let me say that this is why James said, 'Consider it pure joy, my brethren, when you face trials of many kinds'. When you get to Heaven, and you see those who receive a great reward, you may wonder, 'Well, why didn't I get that?' God will say, 'Remember that trial I gave you? You blew it. You just griped, you complained, you murmured. You just said, Why does this have to happen to me?' God will say, 'I was trying to show you.' And so if there is unusual suffering, which is dignified by your demeanour, I believe it will bring a great reward.

It is worth remembering that God's justice will prove to be the fairest system ever. We are all equal; God is no respecter of persons. Anybody can receive a reward. We are all at square one, as it were, because nobody had a head start.

The most beautiful, satisfying, fulfilling words that I ever want to hear is when God says, 'Well done!' Once in a while, particularly after I have gone through an extreme trial, I feel like God was giving me the results of a minor exam. But you see, what really matters, because I am not there yet, is to think on that Day of days, beyond which no more trials are, you either get the reward or you miss out hearing God say, 'Well done!' I want that, do you?

12

Saved, But Only Just

If it is burned up, he will suffer loss: he himself will be saved, but only as one escaping through the flames (1 Corinthians 3:15).

This statement of the apostle Paul has become a watershed in New Testament theology. It is the clearest possible statement of salvation by grace alone, and not of works.

1 Corinthians 3 gives us more details of what Paul calls the 'judgment seat of Christ' in 2 Corinthians 5:10. Briefly, it shows us four things and all refer to the believer. First, the worthless superstructure shall be burned up: 'If it is burned up'. The second thing it shows is that such a Christian forfeits a reward at the judgment seat of Christ: 'he will suffer loss'. Third, it shows the person described will nonetheless be saved, for Paul says: 'he himself will be saved'. Fourth, he will be saved 'as one escaping through the flames'. The next chapter will be devoted to this one phrase.

The mixed superstructure

As I have described previously, we have the option of building a superstructure of gold, silver and precious stones or wood, hay, stubble as the foundation, as Paul put it in verse 12. We need to realise, however, that in verse 15, it is a generalisation. I say that for this reason: I do not think that any Christian will have erected a superstructure of pure gold and nothing else. We all have the wood, the hay and the straw in our lives. As

I pointed out in an earlier chapter, it will be a mixed superstructure. And so when he is talking about the work that shall be burned, Paul is not implying that some will have erected a superstructure of pure gold and others only wood, hay and straw; he is simply showing that the aspects of the superstructure which were made up of wood, hay and straw will be burned.

The burning of the superstructure

Now there are five things that I want us to see in this verse. The first is the burning of the superstructure. Look how it is put: 'If it is burned up ...'

(i) A Day of discovery

It will be a day of discovery, for on that day we will find out, for one thing, who is saved and who is not. Do you remember how Martin Luther put it? He said, 'When I get to Heaven I expect to be surprised three times.' There will be those whom Luther did not think would be there and there will be those absent whom he thought would be there. But Luther said the greatest surprise of all will be to find himself there.

But not only will it be a day of discovery of knowing who is saved and who is lost, but we will also discover who among the saved will have their work burned up and will suffer loss. Among the saved, I doubt not, there will be a lot of surprises. Some will have a reward whom we thought would not; some will not have a reward we thought would get the reward. And so on the Day of discovery, God's infallible computer will have assessed our works. Some of our works will be converted to gold, silver and precious stones that survive the fire of that day, and some of our works will be converted to wood, hay and straw that will be burned up. The superstructure in these lines is mirrored by the metaphors to which Paul has chosen to refer.

(ii) A Day of disclosure

It will also be a day of disclosure: what it is that was unbecoming to the foundation. Now the foundation is Jesus Christ. All who rest on that foundation are saved; that foundation is propitious. It satisfies the justice of God and all who are on it are saved.

The superstructure, however, may not become the foundation. For example, unbiblical doctrine that we may have held will be burned up. An unbecoming lifestyle that we held on to will go up in flames, and what we did that God was not in will be burned up. And those who promoted themselves to the level of their incompetence, and were in constant fatigue, will find that it was not worth it and it will be burned up on that Day, because it will be a Day of destruction - 'if any man's work shall be burned'.

(iii) A Day of destruction

Now that means good news and bad news. The good news is that the blood of Christ will be vindicated: the worthless work will be burned up. God will keep his word; the worthless work will not be held against us. My sins, confessed and under the blood, will not be exposed at the judgment seat of Christ, and that which in me made a superstructure of straw, will be burned up. God will not let you know about me all that is knowable and that is the good news.

The bad news is that the quality of the remaining superstructure after the fire, will be revealed. The lasting quality of the superstructure, what there is of it, will speak for itself. It will be obvious to me, it will be obvious to you, and I conclude that it is not the works themselves that are exposed - they will be burned up - but rather the quality of the superstructure that survives the heat and the light of that Day of days. We will all give an account of the things done in the body whether they be good or bad. That in me that erects a superstructure of gold, silver, precious stones, will survive; but as I said, that in me that contributed to wood, hay, straw, will be burned up. That is when Christian men and women will openly have the praise of God. As Paul says in the next chapter,

> Therefore judge nothing before the appointed time; wait till the Lord comes. He will bring to light what is hidden in darkness and will expose the motives of men's hearts. At that time each will receive his praise from God (1 Corinthians 4:5).

The ultimate trial

The second thing in this text is that it is the ultimate trial. We examined in the chapter entitled, *The Fiery Trial*, how every trial here below is a preview of the ultimate trial. The main point about this is that the trial below prepares us for more glory and if we did not dignify it God gives us a second chance; and the next time around, if we dignify the trial, we are promoted to another level of glory. But the trial above will be the final test; there will be no second chance.

(i) A Day of total clarification

On that Day all speculation will be over, namely, what it was that God actually said and wanted will not be disputed then. You will not be able to argue back and say, 'But look here, it says over here...' There will be no chance of saying, 'Well, I know that I was right...': you will lower your voice then. It will be a day of total clarification. It will be clear who it was that was obedient, and who was not. On that Day every mouth will be stopped.

(ii) A Day of transparent confirmation

It will be a Day of transparent confirmation of what was obvious. I refer to 1 Timothy 5:24 where Paul says, 'The sins of some men are obvious', in other words, in advance of the judgment. They give you a pretty good idea of what is coming to them, so that when the judgment comes you are not all that surprised. And yet, oftentimes, there is a doubt, and this is why Paul says in chapter 4:5, 'Judge nothing before the time come'.

We may think we know who was unable to be renewed again unto repentance, and I think it is possible that there is a setting-in of terminal chastening in this life. There are some who become stone-deaf and never hear God speak to them again in this life. And that refers to Christians who cannot be renewed again unto repentance, according to Hebrews 6:6. It shows they had repented at one time, but that ability to be renewed is gone. We may think we know who is in that state. I have an idea sometimes - I could be right, I could be wrong, but on that Day, there will be transparent confirmation.

There are those who are taken out by premature death. In 1 John 5:16, we read of the sin unto death. God sometimes just takes out of this world those who wilfully will not listen. He says 'Your time is up'. Ananias and Sapphira are examples of that.

(iii) A Day of terminal chastening
We have examined this fearful topic of chastening in a previous chapter, with its three manifestations: internal, external and terminal. As we have discovered, God used the first two of these to get our attention. But he has terminal chastening reserved; God will do by fire what we would not allow by faith. If we judge ourselves, however, we will not come under this judgment. Now is the time to deal with the wood, the hay and the straw in our lives.

Rejection of reward
Thirdly, in this text there is rejection of reward. Notice how Paul puts it. In verse 14 he says, 'If what he has built survives, he will receive his reward. Verse 15 then says, 'If it is burned

up, he will suffer loss'. What was promised in verse 14 is
forfeited in verse 15.

To 'suffer loss'
The word translated 'suffer loss' comes from the Greek word,
zimeo, which literally means 'to be put to disadvantage'. In other
words, if any man's work shall be burned, he shall be put to
disadvantage. It is interesting that Paul uses exactly the same
word in Philippians 3:8, '... I consider everything a loss compared to the surpassing greatness of knowing Christ Jesus my
Lord, for whose sake I have lost all things'. To put it another way,
'I have been put to disadvantage, and yet I count it but rubbish
that I may win Christ.' What we so foolishly hold on to now
because we count our lives dear, and because we fear we would
be put to disadvantage, will cause us to be put to disadvantage
then. Therefore, it is not a question whether you are going to be
put to disadvantage; it is not a question of whether you are going
to suffer loss; it is only a question of *when*.

If you are one of those who can say, 'I consider everything
a loss compared to the surpassing greatness of knowing Christ
Jesus my Lord, for whose sake I have lost all things', in that
Day you will receive a reward. But if you are one of those who
says, 'I've got to hold on to this; I count my life dear; I want
to have a good time; I want to spend money; I want to do this',
you have received all you are going to get. For those who
willingly suffer loss now will one day receive God's 'Well
done', but those who hold on because their life is so special to
them, in that day will suffer loss.

The consequences of suffering loss
The first thing which we lose if our superstructure is burned up
is God's 'Well done!' - for that is what the reward is. We also
forfeit the highest privilege that will ever be granted in human

history to any person. I want you to consider that for a moment.

Most of us have some peak moment of our lives when it was the moment that was so special - perhaps you witnessed some moment in history and you say, 'I actually saw it'. Maybe you have been presented to Her Majesty the Queen. There are people I have met who personally knew Winston Churchill and they want to talk about that. I have a friend who has gone salmon-fishing with the Prince of Wales. I suppose that was the peak moment of his life.

What should be the peak moment of your life? Well, I am going to tell you: the greatest moment that can ever be conceived is yet to come and that is the privilege of casting our crowns before King Jesus. And for you who say, 'Oh, don't talk to me about reward, crown, prize. Surely that is just encouraging self-glory?' No! The greater the crown, the greater glory given to Christ! And how do you think it will make you feel if you have no crown to cast to him who died on the cross for your sins? What a moment it will be if God grants me to take off my crown and throw it to Jesus! What a loss if we have nothing to give.

We also forfeit the joy that could have been ours in that Day of days. This is why John talks about not being ashamed before him at his coming. What a contrast to those who know unspeakable joy!

Naked acceptance
In this text we also find the certainty that we will have to accept openly, nakedly, God's verdict. We will accept it. There will be no affectation then; no masks will be worn on that day.

(i) No masks
We all wear masks, do we not? I wear a mask all of the time. I do not want to be seen without my mask. I just wear the mask

because I want you to like me. I wear the mask to nearly everybody. I am afraid you would not like me if I took the mask off. But on that Day there will be no masks; no mask of smugness will adorn us; no mask of sophistication will be worn then; no mask of superiority. You will not get away with it. There will be no affectation; there will be no argument. If you survive with virtually a bare foundation, with virtually no superstructure, you will accept without any argument what God judges to be correct.

(ii) No quarrel

And you will accept without raising your voice what God's Word said; you will agree then that the Bible gave you ample warning of this Day. You will recall reading the words in this passage.

(iii) No repression

But on that Day, you will have no argument, and you will be ashamed. How foolish to take salvation lightly! No affection, no arguments, no anaesthetics. I am not talking about physical pain, I am talking about mental anguish. In other words, let me put it like this: there will be no repression at the judgment seat of Christ. Do you know what I mean by repression? It is a defence mechanism; it is the way we deal with pain. We have a way of putting something out of our minds. If I do not like something I begin to use defence mechanisms. I may deny that I really feel a certain way; it is what will cause high blood pressure, what will cause a migraine headache, but we repress it. It is never good, but we do it. Some people intellectualise; some people rationalise; some people sublimate. There are many defence mechanisms people use to avoid pain and it is a kind of anaesthetic, if we do not like what we hear.

But there will be no repression at the judgment seat of

Christ. You will not be able to withdraw from reality; you will not be able to daydream; you will not be able to play games. There will be no withdrawal from reality then.

> Of all the words
>> Of tongue or pen,
> The saddest are
>> 'It might have been'.

The triumph of the Word

But the fifth and last point can be found in this verse: 'but he himself shall be saved'. It can also be found in the words of James 2:13, 'Mercy triumphs over judgment'.

For on that day the straw will be burned up, but you will be saved. Nothing can be plainer than that. Even after the straw is burned, that soul will be saved.

> 'That soul that on Jesus
>> hath leaned for repose,
> I will not, I will not
>> Desert to his foes.
> That soul all hell should endeavour to shake,
>> I'll never, no, never, no never forsake'.

It needs to be repeated that we are not saved by our superstructure.

The truth of the Word

That is the basis of reward. We are saved because we are on the foundation alone which is propitious. So as Jesus put it:

I give them eternal life, and they shall never perish; no-one can snatch them out of my hand. My Father, who has given them me, is greater than all; no-one can snatch them out of my Father's hand (John 10:28-29).

Why? Because 'he who began a good work in you will carry it on to completion until the day of Christ Jesus' (Phil. 1:6).

Why will he still be saved though his work is burned? Because Jesus said, 'All that the Father gives me will come to me, and whoever comes to me I will never drive away' (John 6:37).

Why? Because Paul said, 'And those he predestined, he also called; those he called, he also justified; those he justified, he also glorified' (Romans 8:30). As he wrote:

> For I am convinced that neither death nor life, neither angels nor demons, neither the present nor the future, nor any powers, neither height nor depth, nor anything else in all creation, will be able to separate us from the love of God that is in Christ Jesus our Lord (Romans 8:38-39).

It is a triumph of the Word which promises those that are his can never fall away.

And here is the proof of that: though his work is burned up, he himself shall be saved. Paul says in Romans 4:5, 'However, to the man who does not work but trusts God who justifies the wicked, his faith is credited as righteousness'. It is the triumph of the Word.

'Standing' and 'state'

In theological terms, we sometimes refer to a person's 'standing' and his 'state'. What is the difference between these two? Our standing is the way we are seen by God forensically, legally, as being in Christ. That never changes so that the person who is in Christ is no more accepted fifty years after his conversion than the day after. It is the righteousness of Christ which covers him. That is our standing. Paul refers to, 'the grace wherein we stand'. That never changes and that means the foundation, to use the metaphor of 1 Corinthians 3.

What about the state? That is like a graph which goes up and down. It refers to our superstructure and that changes and is mixed. We have all got skeletons in our cupboards; we have all done things we wished we had not, and on that Day how wonderful it is that it will be a triumph of the Word promised to those who trust in him that they shall never be lost.

There are those who are very threatened by this teaching. There are also going to be those who take advantage of it to their peril. But there have always been some, despite God putting them on their honour, who have been foolish.

Lot's choice

There was a man by the name of Lot, Abraham's nephew. We are told in Genesis 13:12, that he 'pitched his tents towards Sodom'. That means that he decided to see how close to the world he could get. He paid dearly, and he paid so dearly that he reached a state in his life in which there was nothing about him, if you just looked at the bare facts of his daily living, to convince you that he was a child of God. In fact, in Genesis 19:8, there is a description of what he did that I would blush to read publicly.

Nevertheless, Peter describes Lot as 'righteous' (2 Peter 2:7-8). There was not a lot to make us think he was righteous. But he is an example of 2 Peter 1:9: 'he that lacketh these things is blind' (AV); Peter lists, in that chapter, faith, goodness, knowledge, self control, perseverance, godliness, brotherly kindness and love. If these abound in us, we will receive a rich welcome into the kingdom.

The witness of Scripture

But few people have taken notice of verse 9. This is Peter's way of saying that one can be saved, but can lack those things and become blind.

King Saul once said, 'God has departed from me and answers me no more'. But Samuel was to say to him, 'Before sunset tomorrow, you are going to be where I am'. Saul is an example of one who sinned unto death but was saved.

In Numbers 14:20, God wanted to wipe out the children of Israel but Moses interceded and said, 'God forgive them'. In Numbers 14:20 you can read of the outcome for that generation. God says, 'I have forgiven them'. But he says they will not see the Promised Land, and here is an example of those whose work will burned up but will be saved.

Let me recall the words of Amos 4:11: 'Plucked from the fire, a brand plucked from the burning'. There is the proverbial expression, 'Saved by the skin of one's teeth' and that is what Paul is talking about here. Well, you may say, 'Such people like that aren't worthy of being saved'. You are quite right; they are not. But are *you* worthy to be saved?

> For who makes you different from anyone else? What do you
> have that you did not receive? And if you did receive it, why
> do you boast as though you did not (1 Corinthians 4:7).

None of us is worthy and it should not surprise us that even those who are saved through the fire are trophies of sheer grace.

Well now, if I understand Paul, the implication is that had Christ come then, at the time he wrote this letter, these Corinthian Christians would be in the category he is describing in verse 15. Therefore you may wonder why Paul brought eschatology into the picture? He did so because it was a way of motivating carnal, childish Christians to grow up. I hope it will do that for us. I do not want to be saved but only just. I want to participate in the crowning of our Lord Jesus Christ.

13

Fireproof Salvation

If it is burned up, he will suffer loss: he himself will be saved, but only as one escaping through the flames (1 Corinthians 3:15).

Fire and the Day of God

The theme of this verse is that of a building on fire, and of one passing through it without being hurt: 'only as one escaping through the flames'. It takes place on God's Day to which Paul refers in verse 13: 'his work will be shown for what it is, because the Day will bring it to light'. Paul adds that the Day will be revealed by fire and 'the fire will test the quality of each man's work'. The reference to the fire and the day of God is not put here in isolation. In 2 Thessalonians 1, Paul says that Jesus will come with his angels in blazing fire to punish those that do not know God. So that the Day itself is accompanied with fire. Indeed, long ago the prophet Isaiah put it like this in his book, chapter 66:15: 'See, the LORD is coming with fire, and his chariots are like a whirlwind; he will bring down his anger with fury, and his rebuke with flames of fire'. In 2 Peter 3:10 this theme is repeated: 'But the day of the Lord will come like a thief. The heavens will disappear with a roar; the elements will be destroyed by fire, and the earth and everything in it will be laid bare.'

Now obviously these verses all cohere, referring to what happens on that Day of days. Paul, borrowing that imagery or reference to fire, says that on that Day of days 'when every man's work shall be manifest' those whose work will be burned up will be saved though it will be 'by fire'. Before we look at the word 'fire', I want to make three general observations.

The Second Coming of Christ

The first is, this is an *eschatological statement* - it refers to the last times. It refers to the Second Coming of Jesus. There are a lot of details not filled in. Paul assumes we know more than perhaps we do know, but he feels that he does not have to say a lot; he has said it elsewhere; so he just makes reference and assumes we know our eschatology. We may not feel that we know it but the point is in this particular verse he does not tell us everything about the Second Coming, it is just almost a passing reference. But it is an eschatological statement.

Behaviour counts

Second, it is an *ethical statement*, because it shows that our conduct matters: 'If it is burned up, he will suffer loss.' It shows what God thinks of conduct that is unbecoming to the foundation which is Christ.

Only by faith

Third, it is an *evangelical statement*, because this is, simply, a vindication of the gospel of grace, through faith in Christ alone. Paul wrote in Romans 10:9: 'That if you confess with your mouth, "Jesus is Lord" and believe in your heart that God raised him from the dead, you will be saved'.

Those who say you have got to have a lot more are shown by this verse it is not so, not for salvation. Salvation - going to heaven and not to hell - is by the sheer grace of God; our works do not help or contribute at all. And the absence of our good works do not cause us to forfeit our salvation for Paul said one would be saved 'so as by fire'.

The explanation of the fire

It will be useful to look at what this verse is not teaching. There are several possibilities that I wish to discuss.

(i) Not to encourage presumption

There will always be those who say, 'Well, it doesn't matter how I live, I'll be saved by fire'. St Augustine, a long time ago, seeing the same implications, warned against presumption so we can see why it needs to be said. As a matter of fact, that is why Paul brought it in, lest we be presumptuous. He was addressing carnal Christians and it was his motive in bringing this passage to bear that it would stir them up; to show that though we are saved by faith alone, as he put it in 2 Corinthians 5:10, 'We must all appear before the judgment seat of Christ'.

(ii) Not purgatory

There may be some who say this verse refers to purgatory, and so I felt that I should take just a brief moment to explain that this is not so. It is important to note that purgatory is not taught in the Bible at all; it goes right against the doctrine of justification by faith alone. You say, 'Well, where do some people get it?' One place is the Book of Maccabees, which is not in the Protestant Bible (It was not in the earliest canon of Scripture drawn up by Athanasius, and it was not even in the Old Testament canon drawn up by the chief rabbis). The Book of Maccabees is in the Apocrypha.

You may be interested to know that even modern Roman Catholic theologians do not see 1 Corinthians 3:15 as a reference to purgatory. Though Roman Catholics may want to believe in purgatory, they would be quick to say that 1 Corinthians 3:15 does not describe it. You can look for yourself in the official Roman Catholic version, the Jerusalem Bible (which is not a bad translation). There you will find a footnote which says, 'There may be some in medieval times that saw this as referring to purgatory, but this does not refer to purgatory'.

But there are other reasons why it does not refer to purgatory. First, it refers to the day of the Second Coming, so it is not a reference to an intermediate state. On that Day it will be complete. Second, it assumes resurrected bodies, not disembodied spirits. Third, the work is burned up, not the person. In fact, the person is not touched at all. Fourth, one passes through the fire in the twinkling of an eye, not through a long period of time. And finally, one is no more worthy after the fire than he was before it, because we are all saved by the grace of God.

(iii) Not punishment

What else can be said about the fire to explain it? It is not punishment - certainly not for the Christian. Now obviously, the fire generally that accompanies the Second Coming is there for punishment as 2 Thessalonians 1:7-8 puts it, 'This will happen when the Lord Jesus is revealed from heaven in blazing fire with his powerful angels. He will punish those who do not know God'. So one has to say that the fire is for punishment, but not for the Christian. That is the point. This fire through which one is saved is not a means of punishment.

But then you have the question, and you are bound to have raised it if you have thought about it very much at all, could the fire be the fire of Gehenna? Gehenna is the Greek word translated 'hell' that we associate with eternal punishment. When we consider the text above from 2 Thessalonians, we have to say that the fire there is probably the fire of Gehenna. When we turn to this chapter's text, we have to admit that Paul does not say and so it is not certain, but if he is talking about the same fire as in 2 Thessalonians 1, it could be Gehenna. It is a fascinating subject and after much thought, I think it could be. In any case, those described in verse 15 pass through it in the twinkling of an eye and so one does not suffer from it; there is no punishment.

(iv) Not propitious

When we come to this point we have to examine the complex world of Greek semantics. When Paul wrote that we are saved by fire, it may seem as though fire is the means of one's salvation. But we know that only the blood of Jesus Christ is propitious. In that case, why did he say, 'saved by fire'? The Greek grammar does not mean we are saved by fire as we are saved by the blood of Jesus. Even in English if I were to say 'I know someone who was saved by Victoria Station' you would not think that Victoria Station had saved him; you would think he had been saved 'near' Victoria Station. And so fire is not the instrument of salvation, it is the reference to how close one was to the fire.

The essence of the fire

Having considered what the fire is *not*, we must look now at what it is. Let us peel the layers of the onion away and get closer. What is the fire?

(i) Metaphorical fire

There are three ways to look at this: first of all, Paul is undoubtedly speaking metaphorically. A metaphor means that what is said is not meant literally but refers to a comparison. Now fire, as we have discovered earlier, provides basically two things: heat and light. Heat burns what is combustible - hay, wood and straw. Light reveals what is left after the fire has done its work, and if there is anything left it will be because the superstructure was made up of gold, silver and precious stones. It is all clearly metaphorical.

(ii) Metaphysical fire

But, secondly, he may be speaking metaphysically: that it could be fire beyond the physical level. It could be supernatural fire. It may be real fire and yet something beyond the physical.

For example, Moses saw the bush on fire, but the fire did not consume the bush. So that this may be God's fire manifested with a specific design: it burns the superstructure of straw, but not the person.

An illustration that was often used by the Church Fathers is the three Hebrew children who were in the midst of the burning, fiery furnace. They were seen walking, and the only thing that was burned was the rope. And the king looked in and said, 'I see not three but four, and one is like unto the Son of God'. So that the fire revealed who was with them. On that last Day one may be in the fire, passing through it, but Christ will go with us, and only wood, hay and straw will be burned.

Someone may say, however, 'But just a minute, the fire that is referred to in Daniel 3, with the three Hebrew children, Shadrach, Meshach and Abednego - that was literal fire.' That brings me to the third possibility: it may mean material fire for all I know. There is the mystery of 2 Peter 3:10: 'But the day of the Lord will come like a thief. The heavens will disappear with a roar; the elements will be destroyed by fire, and the earth and everything in it will be laid bare.'

(iii) Material fire

Some think that may refer to a nuclear phenomenon - I do not know. We do know however that in the days of Lot, Abraham's nephew, we read in Genesis 19:24-25, 'Then the LORD rained burning sulphur upon Sodom and upon Gomorrah - from the LORD out of the heavens. Thus he overthrew those cities and the entire plain'. And Lot was told just seconds before, 'Go, move, quickly, don't look back!' and that is how close Lot was to the fire.

How then do we look on this event in Lot's life? It says the Lord rained fire and brimstone. Was it metaphysical fire, was it lightning? Much thought has been given to this and archaeologists have shown that there were deposits of oil in the same area where Sodom and Gomorrah once existed. What could have happened was an earthquake and lightning coming down upon the deposits of oil and causing the fire. The point is it *could* refer to material fire just as the fire referred to in 2 Peter 3 could be a nuclear phenomenon.

Therefore, whether Paul is speaking metaphorically, metaphysically or materially, no child of God is hurt by the fire. Leon Morris suggests that the imagery is that of a man who has to dash through the flames to escape to safety, but like the three Hebrew children, they were unhurt by the heat of the flames.

The effect of the fire

(i) Communication

We come then to discuss what it is the fire does. First of all, it communicates; it sends a signal that nobody is going to question. God's Day has come - the Day of God the Creator; the Day of God the Redeemer; the Day of God the Judge. That day has come - the Day of his vengeance; the Day of his wrath.

How 1 Corinthians 3:15 squares with other passages is not our concern here. I do know we are told that Jesus comes with the clouds; we are told he will come with angels; we are told he will come with the sound of a trumpet. But Paul does not give a comprehensive eschatological statement in this verse. What I am saying is that it will communicate to everybody, 'This is IT!' Everybody will know what is happening - it is God's Day.

(ii) Consumption

The fire also consumes that which is combustible - wood, hay and straw. In the chapter entitled, The Fiery Trial, I stated that anything on the foundation which is unbecoming, and which does not fit with the person and work of Christ, will be burned up. I want to consider now what might that be. What might that superstructure be that will be consumed?

Unconfessed sin

When we speak of unconfessed sin, what do we mean? It will be useful to consider David, the Old Testament king, and his adulterous relationship with Bathsheba.

We should note that had David died during the two years before Nathan the prophet exposed his sin of adultery and murder, David would have been saved so as by fire. You cannot tell me that David was only saved *after* Nathan the prophet came to him. No, David was a saved man before. I hope no-one reading this has the guilt of adultery, not to mention murder, on his or her conscience. But I can just tell you this, if it is unconfessed, if it has not been dealt with, your Day is coming.

David, you see, thought he had got away with it. Two years is rather a long time, but then he was sleeping well at nights. All was going well. But one day, there came a knock on his door, and Nathan the prophet exposed the whole thing. Nothing was ever to be the same again for David.

But God gave David, I can only call it a second chance, that is to say his life was not finished. Had David been taken away during those two years after he sinned as he did, he would have gone to Heaven, without a reward. But God says, 'David, would you like to start over?' and David, though it was the downward side of his life, began to trust the Lord again and God used him. Mark it: David will not be saved by fire on that

Day. He showed himself to be a man of God after his repentance.

Maybe you feel that there is a skeleton in your cupboard and there is no hope of a reward in your case. You must deal with that; confess it. Do not go round telling people, but get it right. Stop it! There is time left; thank God you were not taken for, had you been, you would have been saved so as by fire. God has given you time. Thank him for it.

Unbiblical teaching
Any teaching, any association of ideas or any bodies of thought which do not use the Scriptures as their starting point will be burned up.

Undeserved reputations
On God's Day, the last shall be first, the first shall be last. There are a lot of people today that have reputations: God does not like it but he can wait a while; time is on his side. Those who have a high profile, sometimes are frauds and phonies and they have yet to be found out. God says, 'I'll deal with them'.

Unwarranted accomplishments
Maybe you are really proud of what you have done? God says, 'I'm not impressed.' Maybe you have been able to pull off this big deal? God says, 'I wasn't in that.' Maybe you have got through this examination and you just feel so good about it? God may burn it up. He judges what deserves credit and anything which he deems unwarranted will be burned up.

Unbecoming words
Finally, words that are unbecoming feel the fire's heat and destructive power. Every idle word we have ever spoken will cause us to give an account on the day of Christ.

(iii) Clarification

We are thinking about the effect of the fire. It communicates that the Day has come. It consumes what is combustible, but there is a third thing it does: it clarifies. It will show, for example, the last to be first and the first, last. It will show who was faithful. Fire exposes gold, silver and precious stones. It will show those who suffered and kept quiet about it; their day will come. It will show those who were frauds. The fire will burn up the straw and they will be exposed.

Paul says we shall stand before the judgment seat of Christ and give an account of the things done in the body. This is why this study is not going to encourage presumption. You will, in that Day, wish you had paid attention for it will clarify who was on the foundation and who was not. Because it would seem that the fire, 1 Corinthians 3:15, is in some way connected to the fire of 2 Thessalonians 1. What I mean by that is that we see that those who are not in Christ, who have not obeyed the gospel, will be punished with everlasting destruction, but those in Christ will be saved, through the fire.

The exposure by fire

We come to the fourth point that this text calls for: exposure by the fire. And what is exposed is the foundation. For if the superstructure is burned up, all that will be left is the foundation.

Nobody knew the foundation was there

But some people, I suspect, have built a superstructure of wood, hay and straw, and you look at that superstructure and you would wonder if there is a foundation there at all. You may say, 'Surely, they are not saved?'

This is something we have considered before but I want to bring together in this respect the Old Testament examples used earlier: Lot, David and Jonah. Consider Lot: if you could eavesdrop on that conversation between those homosexual men and Lot which we read of in Genesis 19, and heard what Lot became willing to do, you would have said that Lot was not saved. No saved man would make a compromise like that; he's just not saved. Seventeen hundred years later, Peter vindicates him and calls him 'righteous Lot'.

If you had known what David did, committing adultery with Bathsheba, then trying to cover it up by arranging the murder of her husband, Uriah, you would say that no regenerate man would do that and therefore he is not saved. But he prays in Psalm 51:12, 'Restore to me the joy of your salvation'.

If you had seen the look on Jonah's face when God said to him, 'Go to the great city of Nineveh and preach against it....' Jonah ran from the presence of the Lord. You would say that Jonah was not saved. No saved man would run from God like that. But God was not finished with Jonah. So who would have thought that these men were saved? Yet we too have skeletons in the cupboard.

As well as events in our lives which we would like to keep hidden, we have all got imperfect teaching in some area. This is why you should understand that there will be Roman Catholics in Heaven. 'Well,' you say, 'no Catholic could believe in praying Hail Mary, full of grace... How could anybody play about with beads, the rosary, believe in purgatory and be saved?' You are going to find out. There are people who worship in Westminster Cathedral with whom you will spend Heaven.

God knew
The fire will expose a foundation nobody thought was present but God saw it all along. 'The Lord knoweth them that are his.' The fire will burn up all that which was abhorrent. What we saw in others but never in ourselves will be burned up, but the

foundation abides for ever. Those in Christ shall never perish; the fire burns straw and it exposes the foundation. There it is.

So that one person you and I may 'unchristianise' and say, 'He's not saved!' - God says, 'Wait, he is'. And that one whose superstructure may appear hopeless to you and me and we say, 'He's never been converted' - God says, 'Stop it! He will be saved, yet so as by fire.' The question is: What about you? When you judge, when you condemn others, you are in that moment building a superstructure of straw that will be burned up.

The escape from the fire

Even as we come to the last point I want to discuss concerning this text, there may be some of you who still have one question which I want to help to clear up. It is, 'What does it mean through the fire, I don't get it yet?' To add to the difficulty there is a lot of Old Testament imagery. 'I overthrew some of you as I overthrew Sodom and Gomorrah. You were like a burning stick snatched from the fire ...' (Amos 4:11). Zechariah 3:2 says, 'Is not this man a burning stick snatched from the fire?' So what does it mean?

'*Dia*'

To help you understand this we must look at the Greek and we find that where the text reads 'through' or 'by', it is a translation of the Greek word, *dia*. This three letter word, delta iota alpha, has three or four uses. Let me just give you some of them. (Now these uses have for the moment nothing to do with our verse; I just want to show you how it can be used.)

It is used John 10:1: 'I tell you the truth, the man who does not enter the sheep pen by the gate (through the gate), but climbs in by some other way, is a thief and a robber'. In Romans 15:28 (AV), Paul says, 'I will come by you into Spain' - he means 'I will come through you into Spain'. In 2

Corinthians 11:33 (AV) he says, 'I was let down by the wall' - through the wall - 'and I escaped his hands'.

In addition, sometimes *dia* with the genitive means 'during'. In Luke 5:5, 'Simon answering said, Master, we've worked hard all night' - actually a translation of *dia* meaning 'through' the night. Acts 5:19 (AV) reads, 'the angel of the Lord by night' - during the night - 'opened the doors and brought them forth'. So that sometimes it refers to the actual time.

Dia is also used of accompanying circumstance: Acts 14:22, 'We must go through many hardships to enter the kingdom of God'. And sometimes *dia* is used in consequence of, to mean as it does in Hebrew 11:4 (AV): 'Abel offered unto God a more excellent sacrifice than Cain, by which he obtained witness that he was righteous, God testifying of his gifts: and by it he being dead yet speaketh'.

14

How To Live With Yourself

I care very little if I am judged by you, or by any human court;
indeed, I do not even judge myself (1 Corinthians 4:3-4).

In this chapter we are moving further along in 1 Corinthians,
selecting those passages in which Paul most clearly and
explicitly deals with the future judgment. What will be learned
is how eschatological thinking directly affects our outlook in
the here and now. It has sometimes been said, 'Some people
are so heavenly minded that they are of no earthly use'.

But not Paul. In this verse there is a description of a man
who is totally at peace with himself. And this is what the
Christian faith is designed to do: to bring an individual to the
place where he has such inner strength and liberty that he can
make a statement like this, and not be making it up. He is not
trying to impress anybody but is just stating a fact. Now why
does Paul say this? How was he able to say it? And can we come
also to this kind of internal security?

An unwelcome assertion
To put this statement into context, in verse 2 Paul had made a
declaration which for the Corinthians was very direct. He had
just written, '... it is required that those given a trust must prove
faithful'. And this referred to the ministry, meaning his own,
that of Apollos and anyone else called of God. But this was not
what the Corinthians would want to hear because they had

become enamoured with eloquence. They delighted in the wisdom of words, in brilliance, in speech that sparkled with creativity and originality. But Paul was saying that these things were not important; what is required of a steward or minister is that he is found faithful.

Paul knew that such a statement would be quite beneath some of his listeners. He knew how they would react. They would want to reply, 'Come now, we know that there is more required of a minister than that!'. Paul projected, but rightly, how they would react, and that is why he says in verse 3, 'I care very little if I am judged by you'.

He knew they would judge him for that statement; they were already sitting in judgment upon the great apostle Paul. He did not see himself as great but never forget this: it has been history's task to vindicate this man, for the apostle Paul was not regarded as a great man in his own day. He was held in suspicion by many Jewish Christians as long as he lived.

Paul was not cleared of everything while he was still alive; he was not regarded as a truly great man. We see him like that but they did not then. There were small people in Corinth who actually felt that they could sit in judgment on the apostle Paul.

This message is a word that is relevant for anybody who has difficulty in *handling criticism*. Maybe you know what it is to be criticised? Maybe you have had enough? Maybe it is by parents; maybe your father and mother are still doing it even though you have grown up. Maybe your wife is criticising you; maybe you know what it is to live with a nagging wife and she is always putting you down. Maybe it is your husband criticising you. Maybe somebody at the office. Perhaps somebody at university, in college, maybe a friend. Maybe a Christian with some stature criticised you and because of who it is you take it seriously. Whatever the situation Paul shows us how to handle it.

Paul's response to criticism

Paul is unintimidated by the things they were saying about him. Many of us just fall apart when anybody criticises us, or sits in judgment on anything we have done. We just cannot handle it. But Paul is not afraid; he is unintimidated.

The reason is he knew what they were trying to do. They were trying somehow to punish him verbally. Do you know what it is to be punished verbally? Have you ever punished anyone in this way? You are putting them down. Perhaps you are wanting them to feel guilty.

Fear and punishment

But the fact of the matter is that whenever you concede that the other person is trying to punish you, you immediately know that they are acting in fear. In his general epistle, John says fear has to do with punishment. He says that he who is perfect in love, is not afraid (1 John 4:18). So fear has to do with punishment and if a person is trying to punish you, it is their problem; you do not need to be afraid. Paul is just letting them know this. What a put-down it is when they see that they have not rattled him at all. 'I care very little if I am judged by you.'

This does not mean, however, that we should not listen to criticism. We should not ignore it. Proverbs 11:14 says, 'Many advisors make victory sure'. We need each other. But it is sheer judgmentalism such as Paul was receiving that we must throw off.

That means that when anybody criticises you and you are afraid that what they are saying about you is going to hurt you, remember the words of Peter: 'Who is going to harm you if you are eager to do good?' (1 Peter 3:13). Peter also wrote: 'Be self-controlled and alert. Your enemy the devil prowls around like a roaring lion looking for someone to devour. Resist him, standing firm in the faith ...' (1 Peter 5:8-9). Do you know that the way to get the devil to leave you alone is to let him see that it just does not bother you? You resist him and refuse to let him intimidate you. And so that is the first thing in his response to their criticism.

Paul's perception
The second thing that has to be said is that he was just unimpressed. He saw through their hollowness and their superficiality.

Here is something always to remember about what we should know about those who judge us. There are three things: the first is that *they do not have all of the evidence*. We know that God is not finished with us yet in any case. In addition, they do not know everything even in the area where they think that they are in a position to say this or that. They do not have all of the evidence so they do not really know at the end of the day what they are talking about.

We also know that when anybody judges us, remember that they have *disobeyed Jesus*. Jesus said, 'Do not judge, or you too will be judged' (Matt. 7:1). Now, that is a clear statement, and I have tried for years to see any loophole how I could still judge somebody and it would be all right. But I can tell you, after many years of looking for the loophole, I cannot find any. We are just not given permission by Jesus, to judge anybody. And when anybody judges me I know he has disobeyed Jesus.

The third thing is: *the opinion people have of us is temporary*. It is only a matter of time before they will change their tune; they will have to, eventually. And this is why Paul added in this statement, 'It is a very small thing with me that I should be judged of you, *or of man's judgment*'. The word 'judgment' is the Authorised Version translation of the Greek word, 'day'. In the NIV it is translated 'human court', but it is just 'day'. Now what Paul is doing here is setting up man's day vis-a-vis God's Day. In a previous chapter I considered the topic of God's Day: 'the Day will bring it to light'. That Day when we shall all stand before the judgment seat of Christ, it will be God's Day. He will have the last word. In the meantime, it is man's day, when man sets himself in a position where he can judge. But Paul says he considers the judgment of man's day lightly. And so can we.

Remember, however, that this works both ways. When you next judge someone, you will be ill-informed, be disobedient, and eventually judged by God.

Paul's priorities
Paul is unmoved also by man's criticism. He knew that what they thought would not change anything. Their judgment would not make the slightest difference in what really matters. There is an ancient Arabic proverb: 'The dogs bark, the caravan marches on'.

The reason for our panic and why we go to pieces when somebody criticises us, is because we really care more what they think than what God thinks. And so it is a real indictment upon our spirituality when we get so upset over criticism. It means that what they say is having a deeper effect upon us than what God thinks. The spiritual person is the one who can come to the place where he is unmoved by what people say, because the one thing that matters to him is what God thinks. Thus Paul can say, 'Who is he that condemns?' (Romans 8:34).

The next time you are prepared to criticise another person, and you wonder why God does not deal with that person, I want you to ask yourself this question: 'Has not God been patient with me?' Can you recall that time when you were not the perfect example and God continued to bless you? He supplied your needs, he helped you, he was with you, he answered prayer. Things were happening and you can look back later and think, 'Oh, God was good to me, I didn't deserve that'. Always remember, maybe another person does not deserve it either, but God is being good to them just like he was being good to you. If God does not judge them, it is not your job to do it for him. The beginning of greatness is when one is unaffected by criticism or praise. That was part of Paul's greatness.

Paul's reason for confidence

How then can Paul make this statement? You marvel at Paul and say, 'I wish I could handle criticism like that. I wish what people said about me didn't have the effect upon me that it does.' Perhaps you just wish you could be like Paul who said, 'I do not even judge myself.' This is a remarkable assertion. What peace and security he had. But how is it possible?

Know your heart

Well let me say first of all what this verse does not mean. Paul does not mean that he has made no attempt to assess himself. We know that because in the next verse he says, 'I know nothing against myself.' The very fact that he could say that is proof that he had looked at his own heart very carefully. So this is not a verse to discourage self-examination. In fact, back in chapter 2:11, Paul wrote, 'For who among men knows the thoughts of a man, except the man's spirit within him?' And then in chapter 11:28, he wrote, 'A man ought to examine himself.' It is also an apparent contradiction of 1 Corinthians 11:31 where Paul says, 'But if we judged ourselves, we would not come under judgment.' Paul is not going to contradict his own statements so you can be sure he has searched his heart.

Yet it does look like a contradiction between 1 Corinthians 4:3 and 1 Corinthians 11:31. So how do you bring these two together?

Judge
Having looked at this it seems to me that there are three uses of this same word 'judge' in 1 Corinthians itself.

The first use is that it means to discern, to discriminate or to make a distinction, and that is what he means in 2:15: 'The spiritual makes judgments about all things ...'.

The second way he uses the word is in 1 Corinthians 11:31 when he says, 'But if we judged ourselves, we would not come under judgment'. He is using it there to show that we must be self-critical and deal with any personal malady that we know about. We are to examine ourselves as we are told in chapter 11:28.

But the third way he uses it is in this text and that is to draw a final conclusion, a final verdict. He uses it when he says, 'I do not even judge myself' (1 Corinthians 4:3), because what they had done was to virtually pass judgment on him and it was in essence a final verdict. 'This is what we believe about you, Paul', and Paul said, 'I consider that a very small thing; I don't even judge myself'.

The outcome is in suspense
Well then, why does Paul say, 'I do not pass judgment upon myself'? The reasons for Paul not passing judgment are several.

The first reason is that there is no need to decide *now* who is right and who is wrong. Maybe you are one of those who say, 'I just can't get free to go on until I know whether I was right or wrong in what I did'.

I talked to a minister a couple of years ago who came to me at a place where I was preaching in the north part of England. He said, 'I'm in the worst bondage. I think I've married the wrong woman.' I asked, 'How long have you been married?' He replied, 'Twenty-five years!' 'Well,' I said, 'what if you have married the wrong one? What are you going to do?' He did not know. But he was very serious about it, all torn up.

Paul would say, 'But it doesn't matter. What is in the past is in the past. You don't have to decide.'

Looking back, many of us have doubts about this or that, wondering whether we did do the right thing. I think one of the most interesting discussions is whether or not Paul was right to go to Jerusalem in Acts 21. We read that different people warned him and even Agabus prophesied in the Spirit and said, 'You shouldn't go to Jerusalem!'. But Paul still went.

I have just about decided he was wrong in going. You may say that Paul would not make a mistake but Luke says they spoke 'in the Spirit' and said he should not go. So it looks to me like Paul disobeyed. Now I do not think Paul gave it that much thought, he just said 'I'm going to go'. Looking back on it, however, he could say in Philippians 1:12, 'Now I want you to know, brothers, that what has happened to me has really served to advance the gospel'. So he was not concerned whether he had been right or wrong. He was concerned that the gospel kept going, and that is what he was happy about.

Many of us are not concerned whether the gospel goes on but rather 'Was I right?' and 'What about me...?' Paul said it does not matter. Take the issue when he fell out with Barnabas in the book of Acts. Paul and Barnabas would not even speak to each other for a moment, each was just so sure he was right. Barnabas wanted to take John Mark and Paul said, 'No!' and they just fell out with each other over it. Who was right? Well, Paul would say, 'I do not even judge myself.' Why? Because who knows? The outcome is in suspension. One does not have to know whether one is totally right or totally wrong. Leave it! Leave it to God to order all your ways!

Objectivity for the self

But there is a second reason why he could say, 'I don't even judge myself', and that is because of the objectivity he had of the self. You see, whenever I, R T Kendall, judge myself, I guarantee you I am going to come out smelling like a rose! I am always going to say I believe I was right. We always come out looking good.

This is why the unconverted man, if you ask him why he thinks he is going to go to heaven, says, 'I have tried to live a good life'. He can be the rankest sinner - I have talked to murderers, I have talked to immoral individuals, and they say, 'I've tried to live a good life'. When they assess themselves, they always come out looking good. And even in our converted state, we are going to make ourselves look good. We just cannot believe we could make a mistake like that.

No right to judge

But the apostle Paul had learned a very interesting thing and that is to rise above himself with an objectivity, so that he knew he did not even have a right to judge himself. When Jesus said, 'Do not judge, or you too will be judged', he meant do not even judge yourself, because you are not your own. So when Paul says, 'I can't judge myself', it was his way of saying also that he knew he could not have that much objectivity. A judge is one who looks at all the evidence, but when we come to ourselves we are going to be biased. And Paul knew he himself would be biased. He was humble enough to know not to claim exemption to what Jeremiah said a long time ago: 'the heart is deceitful above all things and desperately wicked. Who can know it?' So Paul is saying, 'I don't judge myself; I wouldn't even trust my own judgment of myself'. So remember this, whenever you judge yourself and you come out looking good - 'surprise, surprise', you would do, wouldn't you? We are all like that and Paul knew he would not be any different - he said, 'I don't even judge myself'. It is an amazing statement.

Overclaiming of spirituality

But there is a third reason why he says, 'I do not even judge myself' and that is the overclaiming of spirituality. There are those who feel a need always to bring in the name of the Lord with everything they do. They always seem to be very spiritual, really pious. Have you ever known a person who prefixes everything with 'The Lord told me this...' - and you just want to go out and shoot somebody! They are just so full of it. It is those who are insecure who need always to say, 'Well, you know, the Lord told me this...' He probably did not!

God's name under attack

This is why we have a statement by Jesus, recorded in the Sermon on the Mount, repeated by James: 'Above all, my brothers, do not swear' - that means do not bring in God's name. Do not say, 'Here's what God told me...', - 'not by heaven or by earth, or by anything else. Let your "Yes" be yes, and your "No," no, or you will be condemned' (James 5:12). For the real spiritual person will leave God's name out of it, because once you bring God's name into it, then no man can say anything, can they?

I was talking to Eldon Coursey recently, formerly General Superintendent of the Elim Church, and I asked him, 'How do you feel about the Charismatic Movement?' The old-fash-ioned Pentecostals have watched the new Charismatic Movement come up, and he said, 'Well, it's painful to see them making the same mistakes we've made.' He referred to a number of things but one thing he said was that when they give a prophecy they always say 'Thus saith the Lord...' He further commented, 'Well, when you say that, you can't judge it, can you? It's got to be; you can't criticise it, whereas the Bible says you should consider it. But if they bring in the Lord's name you just have to take it.'

People use the name of the Lord because it gives credibility so that by it, they are using him. The real spiritual person, however, will set God free because if you do not bring in the Lord's name in that way people can interact with you. But maybe you do not want that. You do not want anybody to criticise you for you want to stand above criticism; so you bring in his name. But remember, real spirituality will leave God's name out on a matter like that.

Openness to the Spirit
There is a fourth reason why Paul says, 'I do not even judge myself' and that is because of his openness to the Spirit. What I mean by this is if I pronounce judgment, my mind is made up and the Spirit cannot show me anything any more. But if I keep my judgment in suspension, the Spirit may have another opinion and once he gives his opinion then it is final.

And we want always to be open to the Spirit. Once you have already decided, God cannot get to you. This is one of the reasons revival tarries. We all are so smug thinking we know it all, so God cannot teach us a thing. We should say, with Paul, 'I do not even judge myself, for if I judge myself I may well prevent the Spirit from judging me and so lose out.'

When we look at Paul, we are seeing a very godly man. And I have concluded therefore, that the more spiritual we are, the less we will pass judgment on ourselves. The less spiritual we are, the more we will be sure about ourselves and pass judgment on ourselves.

The need to prove that I was right, at the root of it betrays a sense of guilt. There is great freedom in abandoning the need to say, 'I was right'. It is a wonderful freedom when you can just leave it. The proof you believe in the sovereignty of God is when you can say, 'It doesn't matter. Maybe I made a mistake. It's done.'

There are words in a favourite hymn of mine which speak of this:

> Pride ruled my will,
> Remember not past years.

The older we get the more we see how in our hasty judgment we went ahead of God and so we missed out. But God always begins *now*. It does not matter whether Paul was right or wrong to go to Jerusalem. Maybe he made a mistake, maybe he did not, but it did not stop the gospel from spreading. And you see, the proof of the sovereignty of God is that he will take us in our mistakes. Romans 8:28 says, 'All things work together for good' (AV). If it had been good, they would not need to work together for good. It is because they were not good that they work together for good. But when they work together for good, we hastily say, 'It means I was right'. It does not. God made it work together for good. And so, if you made a mistake, whether to do this or that, get involved in this or that, to marry this person or that, begin now. God says, 'From now on, watch what I do with your life' and you will find such freedom in not having to prove.

Obviating the Spirit

The fifth point why Paul says he does not judge himself is because it would obviate the Spirit, that is to make his verdict unnecessary. It is to do myself what the Spirit wants to do. This is really showing contempt for the fact that he has promised to move in. And this is why the psalmist said at the end of Psalm 139, 'You search me and try me and know my ways'. Paul had the fear of competing with the Spirit and so confident is Paul that the Spirit will in time give a verdict, that he would just say, 'I do not even judge myself'. This is profound stuff. It sobers me; it is the type of thought that makes you swallow.

Leave it to God

There are two further things which lie at the bottom of this verse and the first is, the utter refusal to defend oneself. Paul says in Romans 12:19, 'Do not take revenge, my friends, but leave room for God's wrath, for it is written: "It is mine to avenge; I will repay," says the Lord.' So at bottom, when you live like this you just do not defend yourself.

Or to put it another way, do not deprive God of doing what he loves to do. Does God ever love to vindicate! He is the expert on it. He has ways of doing it that you could not dream up if you had a thousand years to plan. His way are past finding out. And he promises to do it.

In addition, do not deprive yourself of the joy of watching God do it. He does not want your help. If you start helping he will back off and just wait till you have finished. Sometimes it takes years because you are still trying to do it, and God is not going to do it. When we finally say, 'OK, Lord, you do it,' God says, 'Are you sure? You want me to do it?' Only when we ask him to do it will he say, 'All right. But you be quiet. Stay out of it. Watch me do it.'

Man's uncertainty

The second thing which is even more profound is the refusal to believe that I am right. You may need time to absorb this, but this is why we can say, 'He is all my righteousness'. There is nothing that we can really be sure of in ourselves whereby we can say we know we are right. We find peace when we get to the point where we do not need the verdict; we can just let it lie to all appearances unresolved. Of course, it is one thing to keep quiet about it. It is another that you do not even *believe* that you are right. Paul says, 'I don't know anything against myself but that doesn't make me right!' He has not decided that he was right. He cannot be sure so he lets the past go. This is a complex and powerful conclusion to reach. We will explore it further in the next chapter.

Perhaps you are saying, 'I wish I could live like that!' Here is a man who is free; here is one who can live with himself. He can handle criticism and he can make this statement. Do you wonder how you can be like that? It can be ours if we really believe that God is sovereign and that he has got a plan and is at work. We are told, '... for it is God who works in you to will and to act according to his good purpose' (Philippians 2:13). So God says, 'Relax!' He wants to set us free, so you give yourself a break. You do not have to pass judgment on yourself. Paul's example sets us free.

15

Getting To Know Yourself

My conscience is clear, but that does not make me innocent.
It is the Lord who judges me (1 Corinthians 4:4).

This is not an easy verse with which to deal. We are in a rather
difficult section here and it contains complex and profound
truths.

Conscience
The phrase 'I know nothing by myself (AV)' was an archaic
way of saying 'I know nothing against myself'. We can look
at old English literature back in the 17th century and even in
Shakespeare, and we would find that they would use the
expression, 'I know nothing by him', meaning 'I know
nothing against him'. However, it should read, 'I know
nothing against myself'. In fact, the Greek verb is a word that
refers to conscience. Indeed, it is the verb form of the noun
which would mean 'conscience' and this is the only time in all
of Paul's writings that he uses this word. Because of this the
NIV translates it: '... I do not even judge myself. My conscience is clear ...'

This word, the verb form of the noun for 'conscience', is
used three times in the book of Acts: one example is Acts 5:2
where it is used in reference to Ananias and Sapphira who kept
back part of the price. The Authorised Version says, 'his wife
also being privy to it' whereas the NIV translates it that she had

full knowledge of what he was doing. The essence of it is that it refers to conscience. They were conscious of what they were doing, having full knowledge of it.

A temporary verdict

Paul then had searched his heart and had in some sense judged himself. There are three things about this verse, and they fit neatly into the phrases of the verse, that I want to explore. Firstly his verdict on himself was a temporary one: 'I know nothing about myself'.

Paul clearly took his critics seriously. What I mean is that Paul thought it serious enough to bother mentioning it. Even though he says, 'I care very little if I am judged by you' it was important enough that he admitted that he had thought about it. And so he did feel it. It is important to remember that sometimes critics will be right. They may not be right always, but many times our critics are right or have a point and it is wise to listen to them.

However, what they were doing was judging his apostleship. They were judging him as a minister. They were judging his leadership, his stewardship and it is the area of their attack that he has in mind. He does not mean that he is faultless when he says 'I know nothing against myself'. He is not saying 'I don't have any sin, I don't have any faults'. John said in 1 John 1:8, 'If we claim to be without sin, we deceive ourselves and the truth is not in us'. What he is saying is that as a steward of God he is not prepared to agree with them. He says that as a steward he knows nothing that deserves their censure or their harsh judgment.

He is also saying that there is nothing in his heart or life which is conscious rebellion against God's leadership. At that moment there was nothing of which he was conscious whereby he was not following the Lord and there was nothing wherein he had been unfaithful, or remiss in proclaiming the whole counsel of God: he knew nothing against himself.

Yet he does not say 'I have never known anything against myself', because we have all had to deal with sin in our lives. We have all had those times when we sinned and there was something against us. But Paul is saying in the present tense, 'I know nothing against myself'; as for the past it is washed, it is under the blood of Christ. It is gone forever and that is the same for us. It is because of this that we can say of the Devil, the next time he reminds you of your past, remind him of his future!

The question is sometimes raised however, 'What if we find somebody really sinning? What do we do then? What if we know they have sinned? Shouldn't we judge?' Galatians 6:1 gives the answer: 'Brothers, if someone is caught in a sin, you who are spiritual should restore him gently. But watch yourself, or you may also be tempted.' You can jump on him and say, 'Gotcha! Hope you feel it, shame on you!' But the way to reach a person is to deal with him gently, put your arm around that person, and let him know you are no different; that you understand how he could come to that conclusion or have fallen into that sin.

Unproved innocence

Paul could say then, 'I have looked it over, what you said and my conscience is clear.' Now we move to the second part of the verse which is even more interesting: I call it unproved innocence. He says, 'That does not make me innocent. I know nothing against myself yet am I not hereby justified.'

This shows remarkable maturity and objectivity. It shows an ability to stand apart from himself as though he were outside looking at himself. Now not many know how to do that. Not many ever do that. It requires such objectivity that you see yourself as another person, and you can examine this person to see what you have been like. And so what Paul is doing is saying, 'My conscience is clear but that doesn't prove anything; that doesn't make me right.' Most of us would hastily say, 'Oh, my conscience is clear, that proves I am right,' but not Paul. For Paul the absence of a known malady proves nothing.

I have had people say to me, 'God knows my heart' (I often want to reply, 'You're sure right about that!'). They normally take that to be their code for justifying their deeds: it is a sort of 'you know, (wink, wink, nudge, nudge,) God knows I am right'. What an awful way, in bringing God's name into it, to try to clear your name! This is what I meant when I said I would come back to the point about bringing in the Lord's name.

The problem is we all want to say, 'The Lord told me to do this...' and we think that is going to give us more authority so that other people are going to say 'Oh, what is it?' But we should not do that for it is taking an oath. That is what James meant by saying 'Let your "Yes," yes, and your "No," no' (5:12). If you have ever done it, and perhaps we have all done it at some point, saying, 'Well, God knows my heart', stop doing it! It shows childishness, immaturity and it shows you are protesting too much, because when you are really free you do not have to bring the name of God into it. And so Paul just says, 'That does not make me innocent.'

Self-righteousness

It is the easiest thing in the world to be self-righteous. I have not heard of any course in O-levels or A-levels or university on how to be self-righteous. Nobody needs instructions on how to be self-righteous just as a new baby does not need a course on how to tell a lie, because 'we came from our mother's womb speaking lies'. We are born with original sin and part of original sin is self-righteousness. We have all got that propensity. It will always be there and sometimes the more godly we are, we do not realise, that though we may have conquered the sins of lust and jealousy, self-righteousness has not been conquered. Even in our moment of wanting to be the most godly, there is often in parallel with it: self-righteousness. We think it is a sign of spirituality yet sin has reared its ugly head once again. The heart is deceitful above all things, desperately wicked, who can know it?

An ambivalent statement?

You may be amazed that Paul can talk like this: 'I don't know anything against myself but that doesn't acquit me' as one version translates it. So how could Paul say in one breath, 'I don't know anything against myself' and turn around and say 'but that doesn't clear me'?

(i) the unknown

First, it is because he knows that he has not seen everything that is there. Not everything knowable has been brought to light. It is like a judge who sits on the Bench, and when he hears one side of the argument, says, 'It looks like it's got to be this way'. But then there is another side, there is more evidence and he says, 'Ah, that puts a different picture on it', and then he wants to know if there is yet more evidence. You see few of us could be judges in the courts of law today, because we tend as soon as we hear something, to say 'Well, there it is'. As soon as we hear something we believe it, especially if we like it. It is a very unusual person who just waits until he gets all of the evidence. Paul is being this way about himself. He is standing apart from himself and saying, 'My conscience is clear but I don't have all the evidence' and that is why he can say, 'That doesn't make me innocent'.

(ii) forgotten facts

The second reason he said, 'I know nothing against myself and yet that doesn't make me innocent' is that he knows he could have forgotten a lot. Because we have all got original sin, we tend to forget anything painful. This is called 'repression' in psychology. We are unaware we do it, but we just put anything painful down into our subconscious. That way we do not have to deal with it. It is a way of forgetting. We have a way of forgetting the most awful things we have done.

Remember that David when he committed adultery and then committed murder, possibly got away with it for two years. We do not know what happened during those two years, though we shall find out, I dare say, in heaven. But I am going to make a prediction that for two years David was able to go on with business as usual. He was able to do things, to rejoice in the Lord, I am sure even that he worshipped. He felt good. It would not surprise me at all that for a couple of years he just went on because he felt that God's hand was on him. So when Nathan the prophet came to him and started to relate to him the parable of the two men in a city, one rich and one poor. David was nodding his head. It did not even cross David's mind that Nathan was talking about him. He had forgotten what he had done.

Paul said, 'I know nothing against myself but that doesn't make me innocent', because maybe he had forgotten something. It is too painful to think about. But he has enough objectivity about himself to say, 'I'm not going to say I am innocent'.

(iii) illusions about self

The third reason he could say this was that he knew full well what his capabilities were. Do you? Do you know what you are capable of? Martin Luther said, 'I fear my own heart more than

the Pope and all his cardinals'. He was alive to the dangers it
could hold. But sometimes the only way we grow in grace is
when we are made to look at that which we have forgotten; to
refuse to consider because all the evidence was not in; and to
realize the imperfections of our full capabilities.

(iv) the power of emotions

The fourth reason why Paul would not claim innocence even
though he said, 'I know nothing against myself' was because
he knew how God's presence can make us feel real good, and
so we assume that all is well with us. We can go to church, sing
the hymns, feel his presence, and think, 'Mmmm, I've never
felt so good in all my life' and hastily conclude that therefore
there is no defect in us. God's presence almost always makes
us feel good. I say 'almost' because sometimes we have an
Isaiah 6 experience, where Isaiah said, 'Woe is me!' Other
times he knows how much we can bear and that we just need
to be blessed and encouraged and comforted, but we would not
be right in thinking that those moments prove all is well.

(v) the whole truth

The fifth reason Paul said, 'I know nothing against myself but
that doesn't make me innocent' was that God may decide to
unveil something tomorrow in his timing, that he just has not
unveiled today. It is like peeling the layers of an onion and you
find out there is more, and you think, 'Oh Lord, why are you
only telling me now?' He is so patient. He is so kind. He is so
sensitive. You may have opinions today which God would
show to be invalid by revealing something tomorrow.

Did you ever have a physical examination and you got the
all-clear sign from the doctor, but then he says that there is one
more examination you ought to have, or one more X-ray, and
then it comes out. Or take when David said to Nathan the

prophet, 'I want to build a temple for the Lord' and Nathan just said, 'Do what is in thine heart. God is with thee.' Nathan went on his way and David was so excited. God woke up Nathan and said, 'You've got to go back. I didn't tell you to say that.' Even Nathan the prophet had to wait, and he had to say to David, 'Sorry.'

That is the point I want to make. God may decide to unveil something new tomorrow. We must be careful that we do not hastily conclude that all is well just because you feel fine today. God may have something to say to you tomorrow.

Something happened to me recently which taught me this clearly. I met a man I had heard about. He was a man of whom I had been critical and when I met him I felt so ashamed of the things I had said about him. I knew I had been wrong. As we talked I became more convinced that I was in the presence of an unusual man, a man to whom God has given a gift of being able literally to see into people's lives and speak God's truth concerning them. So I began to say to him, 'Well, now, hold back nothing from me.'

We met several times in the week following that first meeting and all he told me was positive. It was wonderful. I loved it. At the end of that week, however, as I was driving him home after a service, he said, 'I've got something to say. I hope I don't offend you.' What he said was exactly what I needed. This is why Paul said, 'My conscience is clear, but that doesn't make me innocent.' Tomorrow the Lord may show you something new.

Letting God be himself

The next phrase, 'It is the Lord who judges me', I call that letting God be himself for it is he who judges me. Not only does Paul not claim to know everything about himself, or every-thing God's up to, he also does not propose to know what God is thinking. He therefore refuses to conclude that because his conscience is clear it vindicates him.

The truth is, God has enough on all of us to bury us. It does not matter who we are. I do not care how many haloes are over our heads today. God has enough on every one of us to finish us, if he wanted to do it. He is the Judge; he is the one who decides for judging is his prerogative alone.

The witness of Scripture
I want to finish this chapter by quoting three Old Testament passages which show promises of judgment.

> Do not show partiality in judging; hear both small and great alike. Do not be afraid of any man, for judgment belongs to God. Bring me any case too hard for you, and I will hear it (Deuteronomy 1:17).

> Be happy, young man, while you are young, and let your heart give you joy in the days of your youth. Follow the ways of your heart and whatever your eyes see, but know that for all these things, God will bring you to judgment (Ecclesiastes 11:9).

> For God will bring every deed into judgment, including every hidden thing, whether it is good or evil (Ecclesiastes 12:14).

It is comforting to know that if somebody is judging you, you can say to them, 'You're not my judge, God is.' They cannot judge; only God alone can do that.

To be able to say, 'I know nothing against myself' may or may not be a good sign. What we must learn to do is to stand above ourselves so that we will not compete with his verdict now, lest we be shamefully embarrassed later.

16

Wait and See

Therefore judge nothing before the appointed time; wait till the Lord comes. He will bring to light what is hidden in darkness and will expose the motives of men's hearts. At that time each will receive his praise from God' (1 Corinthians 4:5).

This is one of my favourite verses on one of my favourite subjects: vindication. Not only is it one of my own favourite subjects but from feedback I have received in other places over the years, I have discovered that I am not alone. This is something that gets to the heart, close to the heart of hearts, of many, many Christians.

A God of justice
It is close also to the heart of God, because if you did not know, the God of the Bible is essentially a God of justice. One of the early verses in the Bible, pertaining to his justice, is that where Abraham saw that Sodom and Gomorrah would go up in flames, apparently without any warning, and he did not understand it. He knew that God is a God of justice, that he delights in justice, and that he wants to bring justice, so Abraham could not understand why Sodom and Gomorrah would go up in flames without any warning. In Genesis 18:25, Abraham said, 'Will not the Judge of all the earth do right?'

This is a great verse and one that should make each of us lower our voices whenever we begin to question why God does this or that or allows this or that, or, for example why there is the teaching of eternal punishment in the Bible.

In Deuteronomy 32:4, we read, 'He is the Rock, his works are perfect, and all his ways are just. A faithful God who does no wrong, upright and just is he'. And later on in the same chapter, Deuteronomy 32:35, we read of God saying, 'It is mine to avenge'. This is why you have the quotation in Hebrews 10:30 and Romans 12:19.

I cannot help but call attention to the fact that in the same verse in Deuteronomy, 'to me belongeth vengeance and recompense' are these words, 'Their foot shall slide in due time'. This was Jonathan Edwards' text when he preached on the theme, 'Sinners in the hands of an angry God' at the very height of the Great Awakening in the 18th century in New England. He knew that God delights in justice, more than anything. This is the area of his expertise.

If I may put it this way, what God does best is vindicating. He loves to put things right in the eyes of everybody. Let me ask you a question: Do you see injustices? So does God. Do you see unfairness? God sees it. Have you been the victim of injustice? Do you know what it is to have somebody walk all over you to reach where they are and you think God does not do a thing about it? Do you see things going on that you know are not right, and you think, 'God, why?' God sees. He sees it more than you do, and feels it more than we ever can.

Having come under the criticism and judgment of the Corinthian Christians, Paul is advocating in verse five that we must wait and see. He looks forward to the time when all voices will be lowered and every mouth will be stopped. God will have his Day and give the verdict that comes from heaven. Then there will be no higher court of appeal!

For the question this verse begs is: Who really has got it right? We see things in the world and in the church today which makes us wonder what is happening; who has got it right. There are those who have their causes; their movements, and they all say, 'God is on our side', and 'This is what the world needs to hear'. Not everybody can be speaking for God. Who is right? Who is really walking in the light?

These are questions we may want to ask but we must keep in mind that when we ask the questions the jury is out. In the meantime, we may say, 'Ah, our cause is the one that God is behind, because we are upholding the truth' and we can amass many reasons why we are the ones that speak for God. The truth is that the jury is out and we should just wait, because there will come a time when speculation is over.

Plea for a suspended verdict

There are three major things which I want to consider in this verse. The first is that Paul is saying, 'There is no hurry. Why do you feel the need to judge me? I don't even judge myself.' And so, we are to wait. That however, means to stop judging. In a previous chapter the word, 'judge' was shown to have three meanings; and in 1 Corinthians 4:5 it means 'the final verdict'. Paul is saying therefore that we are to stop thinking that we have come up with the final verdict.

Disobedience to this word of God will naturally cause us to begin judging again. I have mentioned it elsewhere but I will mention it again, I think the hardest thing in the world that I have had to learn is to stop judging. I cannot say that I have learned it completely. God is not finished with me yet and he is still dealing with me in this respect. I have discovered that the more I stop judging the greater sense of liberty I have. The less judging I do the more peace I get. When I begin to judge I find out later there is a heaviness and that little bit of satisfaction which I got for the moment is not compensation because I feel awful later.

Five truths about judging

There are five things we ought to know about being judgmental and the first is that judging is *speculation*. We simply do not have all of the evidence.

Second, judging is *schismatic*. It will always cause division; you cannot avoid it. Whenever you begin to judge, the church will be divided.

Third, judging is *selfish*. Primarily it is a sign of our self-righteousness. We do not think that but it is, and it is self-serving.

Fourth, judging is *spineless*. No strength of character is required for you to be judgmental, and it shows no taste.

Fifth, judging is *superseding* because you are doing not only what God says not to do, but you are actually doing what God says belongs to him, 'To me belongeth vengeance. Vengeance is mine.' Five good reasons then for taking this verse seriously: stop judging!

Paul is not talking here about hating sin, because that is something we should all do. It is not valid, gentle criticism that he is denouncing. He is talking about finding fault with someone who is threatening you, someone who is giving you problems, or perhaps someone who just 'gets your goat'. Sometimes it is a personality clash and you can begin to think, 'Ah this is so important' and make it into some big issue when it is really a personal one. Many times what is posed as a theological issue is nothing more than a problem of jealousy or envy or pride which are purely personal problems. Failing to recognise that, we get embroiled in it and say, 'God's with me' and he is not. It is too common a mistake.

I mentioned already in this book that if you are upset, God is even more upset. This can work two ways: if you are in the wrong, then he is upset *with* you. If, however, you are in the right, then he is upset *for* you. This is a further reason why you must never lay a foot upon his turf. Do not lay a finger in the

area of his expertise, because if it just happens to be that what
has upset you has also upset him, you can be sure he has got
a plan. If, however, what has upset you, has not upset him
except that he is upset with you for being in the wrong, you
would do well to lower your voice. That way if you do not say
anything, when the truth comes out, you will not blush. God
does not want our help in this. Just wait and it will all come out.

Let me remind you that this is what is essential to the
doctrine of salvation. We believe we are saved by what Jesus
did for us on the cross, and anybody who begins to think that
it is what Jesus did, plus what we must do, upsets God very
much. God just says, 'I'm not going to save you; I save those
who put all of their eggs into one basket, who know that all of
the glory goes to God'.

God does not want our help when it comes to how we get
to heaven. We get to heaven because Jesus paid our debt on the
cross. We get to heaven because he shed his blood on the cross.
That blood satisfies the divine justice. God punished Jesus
instead of us. All the glory goes to him. Now if that is true with
the doctrine of salvation, it is equally true with anything that
has to do with justice. So when it comes to God vindicating,
he says, 'Leave it to me'.

Now there is something else Paul means when he talks
about having a suspended verdict: he does not want us *to settle
for a premature victory*. There was a time in the life of David
when this was offered to him. I am referring to what we read
in 1 Chronicles 11:12. There we read that David said with real
longing, 'Oh, that one would give me a drink of the water of
the well of Bethlehem, that is at the gate'. And someone said,
'Let's surprise David! Let's do it for him.' So they brought
David the very thing that he wanted so much. But when he was
given the water he did a remarkable thing - he poured it out:
he refused to drink it. It was not the right time for him to drink

it. For what David could have had there was but a drop in the bucket, compared to what God would have given him later!

And so, sometimes you can drink from the well because it looks like you have won the victory. You want to enjoy your little victory. Far better that you just pour out the water and wait, because the vindication that you thought was going to be so sweet to you was not really being handed to you from God. It was something that could be manipulated. It was not the right time. I would urge you that just because you have a chance to look good, to remember David who wanted that water but when he received it, he poured it out! For God's timing is infinitely better.

The promise of a sure verdict
The second thing we see in this verse is the promise of a sure verdict. Look how it is put: 'Therefore judge nothing before the time until the Lord come'.

(i) the appointed time
There are three things to be seen here: the first is 'the appointed time'. The question is, when is that?

There are two ways to look at it: the first way, the primary way, is that it refers to the ultimate judgment of God. Some day, we are told, Jesus will come. This is what we have learned to call the judgment seat of Christ, and there is no doubt that this is what Paul means. It goes back to verse 13 of the previous chapter: 'Every man's work shall be made manifest for the day shall declare it; the day shall be revealed by fire, the fire shall try every man's work of what sort it is'.

Paul says we must all stand before the judgment seat of Christ and give an account of the things done in the body, whether they be good or bad (2 Corinthians 10:5). And listen to this word from Romans 14:10, 'You, then, why do you judge your brother?' Have you judged your brother? Have you? Paul says, 'Why?' He even says, 'Why have you set at naught your brother?' Have you felt it your calling to discredit a brother? Why? 'For we shall all stand before the judgment seat of Christ.' The appointed time, when everything will be cleared up, is then.

But there is a second way to look at this verse, and to look at it this way illustrates just something of what it will be like on that last day. It is the way God can come immediately and it not be the same thing as the Second Coming of Jesus. Let me show you how this is. Jesus said to the church at Ephesus,

> Remember the height from which you are fallen! Repent and do the things you did at first. If you do not repent, I will come to you and remove its lampstand from its place (Revelation 2:5).

God did come in judgment. So the point is that there is such a thing as a divine intervention in advance of the final Second Coming. It can come in our day.

That is exactly what happened in the account of Ananias and Sapphira in Acts 5. Now the story is this: there were people who voluntarily sold everything and took the money and laid it at the apostles' feet. It wasn't anything they were required to do, but it was something they did. But the trouble was that there were two, a man and wife, Ananias and Sapphira, who wanted to get on the bandwagon, and they said, 'Well now, we want to show that we are doing this as well'. But they kept some of the money back. Like selling property for £20,000 and keeping £10,000 and taking the remaining £10,000 and laying it at Peter's feet. Now it may be that there were those in the church who suspected that Ananias and Sapphira were doing something suspicious. I don't know that they did. When Ananias came and laid the money at Peter's feet, Peter said to him, 'Ananias, how is it that Satan has so filled your heart that you have lied to the Holy Spirit and have kept for yourself some of the money you received for the land?' This is what some today would call 'discernment': the word of knowledge or prophecy. Peter could see right into the life of Ananias, and Ananias was struck dead on the spot. Three hours later the same thing happened to his wife. What does this prove? It proves that God stepped in and everybody could see what the truth was.

Times of revival
God can do this therefore, and it need not be at the Second Coming of Jesus only. Sometimes this will happen in revival. Sometimes in times of great revival there is such an intervention that you often read accounts of people apologising to one another. They could not get them to do it before but there is such power with the revival and such conviction that they know they have to do it. Many times there are stories of people embracing one another, sobbing on each other's shoulders saying, 'I'm sorry! It's my fault!' and the other saying, 'No, it's not you, it's me!' It is beautiful when God comes in and everybody can see.

Yet there are occasions when people resist the Spirit in times of great power. This is the reason you have the charge of fanaticism. When great revival comes there are often weird stories about people who shook: it is because they were resisting the Spirit. Those who shook were exposed because they were the ones that were trying to hide something. Because of this we have to question ourselves whether we really want revival or not. For when revival comes, it exposes hearts. I tell you this, in case you had any doubts about it. For that is what revival will do. Revival can bring about a condition whereby everybody can see what is there.

It can be answered prayer. God can answer prayer in such a way that everybody sees what he really wanted.

One of the great illustrations in church history, indeed in British history, is that of the Spanish Armada in 1588. It looked as though Spain was going to attack England and England did not have a chance. But the people prayed and at the time when it looked like all the English would be utterly and disgracefully defeated, the wind changed and turned everything around. In hours it was the greatest victory of the century and all saw it as a divine intervention. The people from Spain thought God was on their side, and of course, the people of England thought God was on their side. But it was apparent what God wanted in 1588. It was God's intervention to display present justice at his appointed time.

(ii) the awesome telling

It is worth looking at this verse to see what it does not mean. And we must understand that what is brought to light *will not be confessed sin*. Therefore if God has dealt with you and you say, 'I am sorry' and you have repented, then you need not worry. It is said of that sin, 'As far as the east is from the west, so far has he removed our transgressions from us' (Psalm 103:12); you do not need to worry about sin that is under the blood of Jesus. Nobody will ever know about that.

It does not refer either to *temptation that you are resisting*. There is a difference between temptation and sin and maybe you are tempted, but temptation is not sin. If you are resisting it, you do not need to worry about that being exposed.

Neither does it refer to *any weakness that you may have*. You may say, 'Oh, in time of revival I fear that God will expose this weakness' - God does not expose weakness. We are told that the Lord is touched by weakness. We do not have a High Priest who cannot be touched with the feeling of our weaknesses. He is touched with them; he is not going to turn round and expose your weakness.

What then is exposed? I think there are two areas: first, w*hat Satan was behind*, what he was doing; what will be shown up will be that of which Satan was the architect. How do we know that? Because it says, 'who will bring to light the hidden things of darkness'. That is where the devil gets in and where people, maybe Christians, are doing the devil's work. That is possible. In fact, to return to an earlier illustration, it was said to Ananias by Peter, 'How is it that Satan has so filled your heart?' So this can happen to a Christian.

Sometimes the devil can get in the church; sometimes the devil will use people who have a reputation for being godly, and the devil will take advantage of some particular fault and work and cause trouble in a church. And so, that is what is exposed.

The other is *evil motives*. I often refer to the story in Luke 14 where Jesus told the parable about a banquet. He said that whenever you are invited to one, do not act like you are the most important person there. You must not just roll up your sleeves and walk in to take your place at the top table. Do not do that because it may be that the host will say, 'Oh, excuse me, but I'm afraid we've got that seat for somebody else'. Then you will be humiliated and have to take your seat some place else.

The point of the parable is, take the lower seat. Maybe you will be invited to sit at the top table, but if you go to the top table everybody will see your motives, and they will see your pride. They will see just what you are really like. So uncleansed ambition will be exposed. The follow-on from this is that any conspiracy against the Holy Spirit will be exposed. As in the case of Ananias and Sapphira greed will be exposed. Similarly, uncontrolled lust will be exposed as will jealousy.

(iii) an authoritative testimony

There is a positive side, however, and that is *what is of God comes out*. Who is walking in the light comes out because not only is it an awesome telling, it is an authoritative testimony, 'Each will receive his praise from God'.

At present, perhaps, you have sought praise from man. Maybe in the meantime you just wanted people to agree with you; you could not wait until God stepped in. You wanted everybody to agree with you now. Is it not going to be embarrassing if you get people to agree with you and then the truth comes out, and you find that was not where God stood at all. This is why Jesus said, 'How can you believe if you accept praise from one another, yet make no effort to obtain the praise that comes from the only God' (John 5:44). But in the appointed time there will be an authoritative testimony: it won't be you trying to get people to your side of things. God himself says, 'I'm going to give my opinion'. It will be God's own opinion which will be unveiled.

The promulgation of a satisfying verdict

When the time comes God will judge in such a manner that everybody will see and it will be a satisfying verdict. Think for example, of Stephen. He was considered to be a heretic and was stoned as a result. If you had been present and you had seen Stephen before the Council, you would have seen his face aglow and that is a pretty good hint that the anointing of God was on him. But not all saw it. Then at the end, when they were stoning him he said, 'I see Jesus' and that made them madder than ever. If you were a Christian, you would have a good idea of where God stood. Nobody else saw it; they screamed and gnashed their teeth at him. But one day, all of them will see that Stephen was anointed of God, and that is where God stood.

If you had been present at the martyrdom of Polycarp in 150

AD, when he was burned at the stake, you would know God's opinion of him then. He was asked one more time to deny the Lord and praise Caesar. His brave reply was, 'Eighty and six years have I served him and he has done me no wrong. How can I deny my Lord and my King now?' He said, 'Light the flame', and they did. At the very moment when the flames were to take over Polycarp's body, Christians present in the Coliseum witnessed the most unusual phenomenon - a wind suddenly came into the stadium and the flames encircled Polycarp's body but they were not even touching him.

That was a pretty good hint as to where God stood. But those who were angry did not see it that way and so in their anger they took a spear and thrust it into Polycarp's side, and the blood and water gushed out and put out the fire.

Polycarp died, but there will come a day when nothing will be hidden. It is the day of judgment that we must fear. It is a tragic thing to be caught out like Ananias and Sapphira were. David committed adultery, then murder, and got found out; but there are people who commit adultery who never get caught. Jonah ran from God; he was found out. Some run from God; they do not get caught.

But you see, the promulgation of a satisfying verdict is when it all comes out. This is why, if you are found out now, it is wonderful. This is why at the Lord's Supper Paul says, 'But if we judged ourselves, we would not come under judgment'. If we deal with it now, it will not be brought up then. If we do not, in that Day it will be awesome. It will be a satisfying verdict when everything comes to light.

It is satisfying also in another way: *it will be worth waiting for*. John gives us a glimpse of what will be the Christian's lot: he 'saw under the altar the souls of those who had been slain because of the word of God and the testimony they had maintained. They called out in a loud voice, "How long,

Sovereign Lord, holy and true, until you judge the inhabitants of the earth and avenge our blood?" '

God knew how much they could bear, and we are told that white robes were given to every one of them. You see, there is coming a day when God shall wipe away all tears. There will be no more death, nor crying, nor pain for the former things are passed away (Rev. 21:4). It will be worth it all when we see Jesus. Life's trials will seem so small when we see him.

And so, on that day, at the judgment seat of Christ, let me give you a tip, be on the lookout for those who suffered, who were stepped on, who were lied about, and kept quiet. Men who refused to drink of the well of Bethlehem, and who said, 'I'll just wait and see how God handles it; I'm not even going to taste of the water, pour it out'. More satisfying than the coolest stream will be when God gives you his water which he has prepared for you to drink.

When it comes to this matter of passing of final verdict, God gives strict orders to us all: *wait and see*.

17

God's Anger Towards Immorality

Even though I am not physically present, I am with you in spirit.
And I have already passed judgment on the one who did this,
(sexual immorality), just as if I were present. When you are
assembled in the name of our Lord Jesus and I am with you in
spirit, and the power of our Lord Jesus is present, hand this man
over to Satan, so that the sinful nature may be destroyed and his
spirit saved on the day of the Lord (1 Corinthians 5:3-5).

The purpose of this chapter - my treatment of the above verses
- is to show two things. First, how it is possible to be saved by
fire at the judgment seat of Christ. For the man who had
engaged in sexual immorality with his step-mother (1 Cor.
5:1) was obviously a Christian. Had he not repented - but
which thankfully he did - he would have been an example of
one saved by fire: terminal chastening. Secondly, Paul's
horror that this actually happened mirrors how grieved God
was with the offending man and the church in Corinth that this
situation existed. The man evidently got away with it until then
and the church did not seem to be too bothered about it.

Paul begins this fifth chapter of 1 Corinthians by speaking
forcibly and openly about the reports of incest within the
Corinthian church. He explains that they are proud of it and adds,
'You are proud! Shouldn't you rather have been filled with grief
and put out of your fellowship the man who did this?'

Yet Paul does not attack the man, but the church generally

for allowing this sort of thing to go on. And so, what Paul proposes to do is to carry out his apostolic authority. What they should have done, he now proposes to do himself, although not without their cooperation. The climax of this matter is found in verse 5 when we see some of the most awesome language in the New Testament. 'Hand this man over to Satan.' What an extraordinary thing to say! 'So that the sinful nature may be destroyed and his spirit saved on the day of the Lord.' What authority Paul claims!

This comment of Paul's is firstly an *apostolic* statement. I point this out because I suspect that we do not have apostolic power today. It needs to be seen also that it is a *prophetic* statement because he said, 'I am not with you in body, but I am with you in spirit and I have passed judgment already, and I'm telling you what to do: hand the man over to Satan.'

But it needs to be said, thirdly, that it is a *theological* statement; 'so that the sinful nature may be destroyed and his spirit saved on the day of the Lord.' Some say that this is the strongest verse in the New Testament for the doctrine of the eternal security of the believer, which we call, *Once saved, always saved*. The reason it is regarded as such a strong statement is that here is a situation where a believer's life was not at all what God proposes the Christian life should be, and yet he is granted to be a Christian. Paul looks towards the man being saved in the Last Day. He never questions that the man is saved; he is taking that for granted throughout this section, but what he wants is that this man is irrevocably put out of the church. It is the best thing that can happen to him; it is the best thing that can happen to them. If someone is put out of the church, you are doing that person a favour. And in the case of the church here cancer was spreading right through the body; Paul knew it and he could not wait a minute longer.

What is at stake here is implied power. In 1 Corinthians

4:19, Paul refers to those who were arrogant: 'But I will come
to you very soon, if the Lord is willing, and then I will find out
not only how these arrogant people are talking, but what power
they have.' How then does Paul propose to do this? At the close
of chapter four, Paul expresses this clearly. He says, 'For the
kingdom of God is not a matter of talk but of power.' He is
going to demonstrate power and give a taste of what he means
by power.

The word, 'power', is often used in the New Testament, and
it actually has two meanings, in fact there are two separate Greek
words meaning power. There is *exousia* which means 'authority'
and there is *dunamis* which means 'energy', and here we are
seeing both in execution. I want us to see various kinds of power;
that will be the operative word as the passage unfolds.

Revelatory power
Notice how Paul puts it in verse 3: 'even though I am not
physically present, I am with you in spirit. And I have already
passed judgment on the one who did this, just as if I were
present'. By revelation he knows what is going on in Corinth,
and he says, 'I have passed judgment'. The Greek is in the
perfect tense, which is the strongest possible tense to say that
it is something decided; it is over and done with. I have passed
judgment, my mind is made up; I do not need any more
information. By revelation he knows exactly what is going on,
as if he were right there.

'Judge'
This activity, passing judgment or to judge, has come up a
number of times already. In a previous chapter I considered the
three ways in which it is used in this epistle: to discern or to
discriminate (1 Cor. 2:15), to be self-critical (1 Cor. 11:31),
and to draw a final conclusion or verdict (1 Cor. 4:3).

When we come to this verse in chapter 5:3 where Paul says, 'I have already passed judgment on the one who did this' the question is, is this a new use of the word or is it a way he has already used it? Well, I think the answer is that it is the way he uses it in chapter 2:15, but also the way he uses it in chapter 4:3, when he uses it to draw a final conclusion. He says, 'I don't draw a final conclusion with reference to myself, God does that'; but what he does do is to admit he is drawing a conclusion with regard to the person involved. And there is nothing personal in this - he does not even know the man, but he knows what has happened. He knows too the effect it is having on the church, so he is making a judgment, and it comes out of his apostolic authority.

'In spirit'

One of the big questions that one has to deal with is when Paul says, 'I'm not with you physically, but I am with you in spirit'. To which 'spirit' is he referring, the human spirit or the Holy Spirit? The Greek word is *pneumati* and because in Greek there are no capital letters, we have to decide which it is. Well, in verse 5, when he says that 'the spirit may be saved on the day of the Lord' that clearly is the human spirit. But in verse 3 it is probably both, simultaneously. Many scholars believe that there is both a little 's' and a big 'S' in Paul's phrase, 'Even though I am not physically present, I am with you in spirit'.

He is using this in a way you and I could not do. Often we will use an expression like that. If you are invited to a party but you cannot attend, you say, 'Well, I am not with you in body but I am with you in spirit'. What we mean by that is that I would like to be there, I approve of what is happening there, I hope it will feel like I am there because I love you. And that is the way we would use it. But Paul means far, far more than that. Take, for example, Colossians 2:5: 'Though I am absent from you in body, I am in present in spirit and delight to see how orderly you are and how firm your faith in Christ is'. When Paul says that he is there in spirit, he means that by the power of the Spirit he is right there and can tell them what is going on. It was another indication of his apostolic power.

So it is not a mere token statement, as we would make today; he means that it is revelatory power. He did not need any further verification; no one need tell him anything. He could therefore act from where he was, and so Paul informs them that he need not wait until he comes.

This gives us a hint as to how God feels about it. Paul is exercised and he makes a judgment because God does not like what is going on. For they were in a situation that we, speaking generally, are not in today. There was such power present. Here was a man who had that kind of power. He knew what was happening and he could use his apostolic authority to deal with the situation.

We don't seem to have that today. People get away with all manner of things. Who knows what is going on in the church across the country? I do not know. I use common sense when people come to see me in the vestry. Sometimes I will say something exactly right and they think I have got some revelatory gift. If I have I do not know it. I am only glad when God can use me.

But I wonder what difference it would make in your life, if you were conscious that there was an apostle Paul around who knew what was happening there?

Paul informs them that he is not going to wait till he gets there. He says, 'From a distance of many miles away I have made a decision'. He wants them to make excommunication effective as if retroactively from the past date as though it had been done then. He says, 'You are going to do it right now. The situation is too serious to give it one more day. Radical surgery is needed. Cancer is in the body and it is spreading rapidly. Look at the effect it is having on all of you. You are arrogant.'

By apostolic power, then by the Holy Spirit and his authority which knows no geographical boundaries, Paul says, 'As though I were there, you do it.' The Holy Spirit would do in Paul's absence what he would do if he were right there. And this would demonstrate both apostolic authority and power.

Reconstituting power

It is not only revelatory power, it is also reconstituting power. I say this because if they carry out what he has asked them to do, they are going to be able to reconstitute themselves. The grieved Holy Spirit will return to them ungrieved, the body will heal and they will come to their senses. This gives opportunity to the church there to rebuild. It lets them realise that they are in such a mess because they have become arrogant, and so unspiritual, and they have an opportunity to repent and rebuild. Thus by apostolic power, then, it is not as though Paul by remote control pushes a button and automatically the man is handed over to Satan. No, he says, 'When you are assembled together in the power of the Lord Jesus, you do this...' Apostolic power needed to be ratified and that brings us to the third point.

Ratifying power

It was something they had to do. This is very interesting. If Paul had done it by remote control, then it would have been done even before they got the epistle to read it. He would have just carried it out as soon as he heard and it would be done. Apostolic power does not work that way. Apostolic power still needed the ratification of the people that were under this apostle. No man of God can do anything by himself; Paul was not a pope. There never has been and there never will be a pope in the church of God. Paul has made a decision but he also has told them what they have to do.

Four things had to occur before the excommunication could take place. The first was that they were to be 'assembled'. This shows that the letter is being read by someone who has some authority in the church - it is not a letter which will be read for the first time to everybody. Paul says, 'when you are assembled', so obviously they are not assembled yet. Secondly, they were to act in 'the name of the Lord Jesus Christ'. What that means is that they will be speaking in the place of Jesus. It is like being an ambassador in another country, who speaks in the name of Her Majesty's Government. And in order to do something in the name of the Lord Jesus, you have got to know exactly what he would do. The third requirement is Paul's spiritual presence: 'I am with you in spirit'. Lastly they needed to be aware that 'the power of our Lord Jesus is present'.

Now why do you suppose, having made this judgment on what they should do, he adds these conditions before the whole thing can take place? Simply because they are going to have to be obedient, and they have got to ratify the authority of this man, Paul, many miles away.

And why do you suppose Paul did it that way? For apostolic power is not automatic. However much authority and however much of the Holy Spirit he had, his hands would be tied if they did not want to obey him. This is the way it is in any kind of institution that God sets up. Take the pastor of a church who can only move as far as the people will let him. Or the husband is the head of the wife, but the husband can only be the head if the wife will let him. And so there must be this coalescing, a coming together in agreement so that what Paul has commanded, they will agree to.

But Paul had a second reason - a most wonderful reason. He

did it to give the sinning man just a little bit of time. He has let it be known how serious this immorality in the church is and yet, by speaking in this way, Paul knows that the word will leak out to the man before they ever gather together to discipline him. He says, 'When you are assembled'; he knows full well that before they all get there, that man will get word of this. There is something tender about all this, because though this is such a severe thing to do, you can see permeating in the whole affair, God's tenderness. He gives the man time to repent so it will not be done behind his back; so that when the church gets together they do not just do it, and then tell him about it later. He is, instead, giving warning.

But what actually happened? We find this in 2 Corinthians 2, and what we learn is very interesting. I think I can tell you exactly what happened. All that Paul envisaged and told them to do never actually took place! It became obvious that the majority were prepared to do it, and it would seem that they have made the offender unwelcome at the Lord's Supper, and told him to stay away. And Paul tells us in 2 Corinthians 2:6 that that was sufficient punishment. He goes on to say in 2 Corinthians 2:7, 'Now instead you ought to forgive and comfort him, so that he will not be overwhelmed by excessive sorrow'.

This should not surprise us. The Bible says that God is slow to anger, plenteous in mercy. Whenever God finally does something like this, you can be sure that such a person had been warned, and warned, and warned, and warned!

One of the most wicked kings in the history of the Old Testament, one that would parallel any wicked leader today, was Ahab. We read in 1 Kings 21:25-26 that, 'There was never a man like Ahab, who sold himself to do evil in the eyes of the LORD, urged on by Jezebel his wife. He behaved in the vilest manner by going after idols, like the Amorites the LORD drove out before Israel'. However when Ahab heard these words from the prophet, he tore his clothes, put on sackcloth and fasted. He lay in sackcloth, he went around meekly and in verse 28, 'Then the word of the LORD came to Elijah the Tishbite: "Have you noticed how Ahab has humbled himself before me? Because he has humbled himself, I will not bring this disaster in his day, but I will bring it on his house in the days of his son." ' Is that not extraordinary? As wicked as Ahab was, because he humbled himself, God says, 'I will modify my punishment'.

Retributive power

How then do we know that the Corinthian church did not hand this man over to Satan? We know because we are to understand that had it happened, the man would never have had opportunity to repent. Once Satan is given total control of a person, he is finished. It is so serious, that according to 1 John 5:16 it is called 'the sin unto death'; you must not even pray for them for it is not going to do any good.

There are, however, extraordinary and exceptional circumstances where Paul could use this kind of language. He uses it again in 1 Timothy 1:20 when he refers to Alexander and Hymenaeus whom he delivered over to Satan. This is language that is to be used very guardedly. I doubt that we have the right to use it, but for Paul to use it meant that though the Christian has the promise that the wicked one does not touch him, that even then Satan does get that person. Once Satan gets him, it is all over.

The reason Paul could say, 'for the destruction of the flesh', is because this was to be the inevitable result. Satan would kill him. It could have been a terminal disease; it could be that the man would commit suicide.

This is what happened to King Saul who, I suspect, is the best example of what we are talking about. In the end he took his own life because there was nothing left in him of any kind of presence of mind. But in this case in the Corinthian church, we know that this did not happen because had they been present, and had the power of the Lord Jesus been there, and they handed the man over to Satan, he would have been finished.

I said earlier that this is the strongest verse in the Bible for, *Once saved, always saved*. Once someone is handed over to Satan they have no chance to repent, and yet they are saved. It is the greatest demonstration of the doctrine of justification by faith alone. You may want to know, therefore, what the Arminians say about this verse. How do they deal with it? What they say is that it would so wake up the man that he would repent, and it was done in order that his spirit be saved. But you see that is missing the point. It is true that all of this could be called shock-therapy; you could call it a way of awakening. But that was not what Paul was saying here, because if the person was given over to Satan, the man would not even have presence of mind to repent. Furthermore, Paul gives no hint that he thought this severe action would have a positive result. Indeed, his comments in 2 Corinthians 2:5-11 show how relieved Paul was. It could have turned out otherwise.

What happened in fact was that Paul gave the man space to repent by the conditions that are outlined in verse 4. He gave the people opportunity to come to their senses. Had they or the man not repented, then obviously we would have a situation where Paul would not pray at all for the man.

Redemptive power

But there is a last point to be made on the subject of power: redemptive power. In 1 Corinthians 5:5, 'spirit' is obviously the small 's'. The words, 'spirit', and, 'soul', in the New Testament are words that come from two different Greek words, *psuche*, or *pneuma*, but often are used interchangeably. I do not want to get into discussion on the relative and parallel meanings of these words here. Suffice to say that the point is that there is a real self, a real person, that survives the body, after the body is dead.

But in this case it is not just immortality; it is not just that the spirit would survive for that is true of everyone. Paul says that in this case, 'the sinful nature may be destroyed and his spirit *saved*'. When? On the Day of the Lord. This man, at some point, had confessed that Jesus is Lord; he believed in his heart that God raised Jesus from the dead.

So when Paul says that the man will be saved in the Day of the Lord, it is obvious that here is a man who will go to heaven. The wonderful thing is that the man, when he heard that this letter had come from the apostle Paul, was repentant. The next time the church got together, this man apparently went to them on bended knee and they held back from delivering him to Satan. They did put him out of the fellowship but they did not hand him over to Satan. The Corinthian church wondered what Paul would say about that. But when the man was sorry, Paul said, 'Quite right, forgive him. He has had enough punishment' (2 Cor. 2:8).

A holy people

Perhaps you have felt that God has been after you. Quite right. God hates sin, and God will not tolerate immorality in the body of Christ, any more than he tolerates schism in the body of Christ. And yet God is patient. He warns. He is slow to anger, so that you can never say, 'God didn't give me opportunity to come to my senses'. As Jesus put it in Revelation 2:21, 'I gave her space to repent but she would not'. God is giving you space.

We can see then how all this validates Paul's doctrine of justification by faith, but, equally, how serious God is that his people should be holy.

18

The Prize Worth Fighting For

Do you not know that in a race all the runners run, but only one gets the prize. Run in such a way as to get the prize. Every one who competes in the games goes into strict training. They do it to get a crown that will not last; but we do it to get a crown that will last for ever. Therefore I do not run like a man running aimlessly; I do not fight like a man beating the air. No, I beat my body and make it my slave, so that after I have preached to others, I myself will not be disqualified for the prize (1 Corinthians 9:24-27).

The concept of a 'prize' from God is a subject that makes some uneasy: the idea of a reward is not a popular one. I will not speculate as to why this matter puts some people off, I only know that it was very important to the apostle Paul.

Selective with the truth
And it is amazing how we can be selective with the Bible. We can be selective with the teachings of Jesus. We often hear people claim to love the psalms but once in a while there is that psalm we read and take no notice of it. An example is Psalm 82 that refers to defending the cause of the weak and fatherless, maintaining the rights of the poor and oppressed.

Similarly, many of us in the Reformed tradition - we love Paul when he is talking about justification by faith, imputed righteousness, sovereignty of God, election, atonement, we love it. But the same apostle Paul was equally driven with reference to this teaching about reward? To put it another way,

Paul was an eschatologically-oriented man; that is, he was driven by what is out there in the future. Paul not only could talk about godliness with contentment being great gain, he could talk about the future. This was the same attitude as Jesus who endured the cross and the shame, because of the joy that was set before him (Heb. 12:1-4).

Why Paul was a Christian

Paul wrote in 1 Corinthians 15:19, 'If only in this life we have hope in Christ, we are to be pitied more than all men'. This is the scripture to use when we meet people who say, 'Ah, if there were no heaven, if there were no hell, I'd still be a Christian'. Paul says, 'I wouldn't! I wouldn't!'

There are those who want to emphasise what is a by-product of Christianity, the fringe-benefits of Christianity. Yes, in this life, we are much better off because we are Christians. But Paul says, 'If this is it, I am not interested. I'm looking beyond.' And so you have those who say, 'I'm not interested in this talk about a reward, about a prize, about a crown'. Paul says, 'I am'. He put it so strongly that he said in verse 27, 'I beat my body and make it my slave, so that after I have preached to others, I myself will not be disqualified for the prize'.

There are two reasons why this subject is important.

Categorization

First, it is important to God for it is his purpose. I would much prefer the idea of having only two categories at the judgment - saved and lost, and if you are saved, you are saved, and if you are lost, you are lost. I would prefer that because it is comforting to think that if you are saved, you need not be worried about being exposed at the judgment for not walking in the light.

Although I find that rather appealing, I do not believe it. Paul did not believe it. It is important to God and yet let me pause - it is a wonderful, wonderful thing to know that you are saved and you are not going to go to hell. There are those of you who may not realise it, that the categories of saved and lost, are what ultimately matter. You either go to heaven or you go to hell when you die. If you go to hell, it will be because you refused to believe the gospel. If you go to heaven, it will be because you believed the gospel; it will not be because of your good works. It will be because you saw that the only way to be saved is that Jesus Christ, the God-Man, paid your debt on the cross, shed his precious blood, by which your sins were forgiven. That is the way any are going to go to heaven.

However, in God's eternal decree concerning his plan and purpose in redemption, there are also two categories among those who go to heaven: those who receive rewards and those who do not. Those who do not will *also* have all *their* tears washed away (Rev. 21:4) - do not worry about their being any sadness in *heaven* because of no reward. But there will be a Day of reckoning when all of us stand before the judgment that *precedes* that entrance into heaven. It is a Day that we are going to live through.

Motivation

The second reason why it is important is because it will make a difference in the way you live. You may say that you do not need that kind of motivation - but you do because this is the way God made us. We are made in his image and no-one is exempt from this. We all need this kind of motivation and when you really do believe this, it will make a difference in the way you live. For this was the purpose of a parable of Jesus:

> When someone invites you to a wedding feast, do not take the place of honour for a person more distinguished than you may have been invited. If so, the host who invited both of you will

come and say to you, "Give this man your seat." Then, humiliated, you will have to take the least important place. But when you are invited, take the lowest place, so that when your host comes, he will say to you, "Friend, move up to a better place." Then you will be honoured in the presence of all your fellow-guests. Everyone who exalts himself will be humbled, and he who humbles himself will be exalted (Luke 14:8-11).

The possibility of open humiliation or open honour was given by Jesus himself to motivate us, and it is in this way at the judgment seat of Christ that the truth of our lives will come out. My congregation do not really know that much about me, but on that Day they will. Nothing will be hidden. So in the meantime it will make a difference if I know that they are going to find out the truth. I had just better live by the truth now.

And so let us be aware of our motives. Part of our reward or absence of it will come from God's plan to lay bare the secrets of man. Jesus went so far as to say, in Matthew 12:36, that 'men will have to give an account on the day of judgment for every careless word they have spoken'. Consider again the words of Paul in 1 Corinthians 4:5:

Therefore judge nothing before the appointed time; wait till the Lord comes. He will bring to light what is hidden in darkness and will expose the motives of men's hearts. At that time each will receive his praise from God.

It is worth considering why Paul returns to this subject in 1 Corinthians 9. Why does the theme of the judgment seat of Christ permeate the whole of this letter, popping up time and again? It happens because the idea of reward on the last Day is never far from his mind.

Notice how he begins this section: 'Do you not know...' This is the Greek phrase, *ouk oidete*. Paul uses it again and again, and it means 'knowledge of a well-known fact'. When he says, 'Do you not know...' it *is because they do* know. Normally he uses the phrase because he has taught them so well, but in this case he is referring to the Games on the Isthmian Peninsula where Corinth was located.

Every two years, fourteen kilometres from Corinth the Isthmian Games took place with competitors coming from all over the Mediterranean world. So everybody knew something of the rules, and their operation. Paul himself was in Corinth during the spring of 51 AD, when the Games were going on. Paul uses them as an illustration of his favourite theme. He says, 'Do you not know that in a race all the runners run but only one gets the prize?' What he does is to apply the Christian life to a race which precedes what he calls the judgment seat of Christ. This appears again in Hebrews 12:1, where the writers says, 'Let us run the race that is set before us'.

Paul uses three important words in this chapter: one is, *brabrion*, which is translated, 'prize' in verse 24. It is used in Philippians 3:14: 'I press on towards the goal to win the *prize* to which God has called me heavenwards in Christ Jesus'.

Another word is *stephanon*, which is translated, 'crown'. It also appears, for example, in James 1:12: 'The crown of life will be given to those who love him'; in 1 Peter 5:4: 'And when the Chief Shepherd appears, you will receive the crown of glory that will never fade away'; and in Revelation 2:10: 'Be faithful unto death and I will give you a crown of life'.

Then there is a third word. It is *misthos*. It is translated, 'reward', and it is used twenty-nine times in the New Testament, fifteen times by Jesus. In fact, this is the word used in Matthew 5:12 where we read, 'Rejoice and be glad, because great is your reward in heaven; for in the same way they persecuted the prophets which were before you'. It is used again by Jesus in Matthew 10:41-42:

Anyone who receives a prophet because he is a prophet will receive a prophet's reward ... And if anyone gives even a cup of water to one of these little ones because he is my disciple, I tell you the truth, he will certainly not lose his reward.

This is clearly then a subject on which the Bible has much to say: it appears again and again and is therefore particularly worthy of our notice.

The possibility of reward

The question we must first ask is, *How do we know that verse 24 does not refer to salvation?* 'Do you not know that in a race all the runners run, but only one gets the prize?' There are those who see the prize as being heaven, being finally saved. How do we know it is not referring to that? Because salvation is *by grace and not by our efforts*: 'For it is by grace you have been saved, through faith - and this not from yourselves, it is the gift of God' (Ephesians 2:8). Salvation, furthermore, is not called a prize, but a gift: 'For the wages of sin is death, but the gift of God is eternal life ...' (Romans 6:23). And salvation is given to all who truly believe, not those who merely start out. Philippians 1:6 reads, 'He who began a good work in you will carry it on to completion until the day of Jesus Christ'. So that when it comes to salvation, it is a gift, handed to us when we trust what Jesus did for us on the cross.

The word, 'prize', is something over and above being saved. You say, 'I don't care about that, I just want to know I am going to go to heaven'. I repeat, you will care about it then. And this is what Paul is talking about. He is saying first of all that it is possible to receive the prize. I think that is wonderful, to think that you will be handed a prize from none other than Jesus himself. Can anything be greater than that? The highest honour in America is the Congressional Medal of Honor given by the

President of the United States. At Buckingham Palace once in a while the Queen gives a similar mark of commendation. The possibility of facing Jesus Christ himself just blows me away!

In addition to saying that not all who are saved will receive a reward or prize, he says that the prize is given to those who run, and who run hard. This is the way he puts it: 'Run in such a way as to get the prize'. There were six categories, for what it is worth, in the Isthmian Games: boxing, throwing the javelin, hurling the discus, racing, wrestling and jumping. Paul refers to two: in verse 24 he talks about the race; in verse 26 he refers to boxing - 'I do not fight like a man beating the air'. In the midst of such stiff competition as these Games would provide, supreme effort would be required.

The prospect of the reward

What Paul does is to compare the Games with the prize at the judgment seat of Christ, and the comparison is interesting. At the Games, all run but only one gets the prize, but in the Christian race, all who run can win. In the Games, athletes compete with each other, but in the Christian race, we are fighting against the world, the flesh and the devil, not against each other. In the Games, only the athletic and the talented dare apply and they are the ones that would get the reward at the end. But in the Christian race, all who want to be like Jesus can receive this prize. In a word, every single Christian can receive this prize; there is no competition whatever. Not a single one of us has a head start; all those who dare, win. We are God's SAS.

The Greek is literally translated 'Run in this way in order that you may obtain' and the NIV says, 'Run in such a way as to get the prize'. Notice the words of action in verses 24-27: 'run', 'fight', 'beat'. Such endeavour is not required in order to get to heaven, but it is required to receive the prize.

The preparation of the reward
The parallel with the Games continues as Paul writes in verse 25, 'Every one who competes in the games goes into strict training. They do it to get a crown that will not last; but we do it to get a crown that will last for ever'. In the Games an athlete was subject to disqualification if he did not go through ten months of strict training.

Self-control
It is interesting that in those ten months the athlete had to do away with lawful pleasures. The Greek word that is used here is *agnoidzo*, it means 'to agonise'. It means self-control in all things, and so the implication is that if the athlete has to have self-control for ten months prior to the games, so this Christian race is to be run throughout a life-time of self-control. This refers, of course, not merely to the body, but to the whole man, body, mind, spirit, and the preparation takes place day and night, fifty-two weeks a year.

The fairness of the competition
But there is something else here. Jesus said, 'To whom much is given, shall much be required' and James said in James 3:1, (this is a verse that I don't particularly like!), 'Not many of you should presume to be teachers, my brothers, because you know that we who teach will be judged more strictly'. Let me tell you the principle here. It is rather like a game of golf. When a golfer who is not so good plays a professional, for instance, he is given what is called a 'handicap'. He has a start on the professional who can easily do par without that lead.

The point is that all are in the same position. Jesus told a parable of servants receiving different talents according to their capabilities. But what is evident is that the man with one talent can receive the same prize as the man with five talents because Jesus made it clear that the prize was hearing the words, 'Well done!' That is the reward.

Resistance to temptation
This is the first element in the preparation for the reward. It is resisting even when nobody can see you. This is what Paul meant in verse 27 when he said, 'I beat my body and make it my slave so that after I have preached to others I myself will not be disqualified for the prize'.

Reaction of the tongue
This is also part of the preparation. It is linked to self-control we mentioned earlier and comes into play when you are tempted to retort, to indulge in gossip or to discredit someone.

Response to trial
Remember that God is watching to see our responses. And it works both ways. When you murmur or complain, God takes notice. When you dignify it, God takes notice then, too.

Refining of the talent
Preparation for the reward involves hard work and diligence. Verse 25 says, 'Every one who competes in the games goes into strict training'. If you care about reward, you care about refining your talent, about discovering your gift and improving it.

Rigour of training
Knowing all the ways to act and things to say is useless unless we put our theory into practice. We have to both know the Word and apply it. Thus verse 26 reads, 'Therefore I do not run like a man running aimlessly; I do not fight like a man beating the air'.

Perhaps that involves memorising Bible verses. That is an
art that is perishing from the earth. Since I have been minister
in Westminster, it was my privilege to preach at the funeral of
a lady who was 100 years of age, who still was memorising a
new verse every day. But that is something people do not do
any more.

Or perhaps it means attending a Bible study regularly, or
being diligent in Bible study and prayer. Why do we have to
do these things? I will tell you why: 'Every one who competes
in the games goes into strict training. They do it to get a crown
that will not last, but we do it to get a crown that will last for
ever.'

The permanence of the reward

The prize won at the Games was a wreath, sometimes made of
pine, and strangely enough, sometimes made of celery! That
is right! Can you imagine wearing a wreath of pieces of celery?
Perhaps, if it is fresh and you give me some salt with it I could
enjoy it.

The wreath was already beginning to wither when they put
it on the winner's head. So when Paul says they do it to get a
crown that will not last, that sounds like a British understatement. But what it looked like is not the point. The winner had
no thought of the composition of the crown. As with modern
athletes, victory meant fame; it was for prestige and sometimes
fortune, so that the crown was simply a symbol of victory.

But, says, Paul, that crown was nothing, nothing in the light
of the believer's prize. Who knows what it will look like? Who
knows whether it is a symbolic gold crown or if it is literal?
Who knows? But just to hear the words of Jesus, 'Well done!'
will give to that person a self-consciousness that will last for
ever.

Revelation of the truth
Whether literal or symbolic the crown will be based upon three things: first, the revelation of the truth. For that is all it's going to be. You are not going to get what you do not deserve. For example, Philippians 2 talks about God highly exalting Jesus and giving him the name which is above every name. But we are told Jesus was God from the beginning. At the end everybody recognizes him as God. It was not something new. What happens at the end is that what comes out is what has been true all along. It will all come out.

The recognition of the task
At the judgment seat of Christ it will be plain to see also whether what you did took effort, or whether it came naturally. What will come out then is whether you fulfilled the task God gave you to fulfil which required going beyond the call of duty. You will not receive reward for simply putting in the hours. Effort is required. We are commanded to run, not merely crawl.

The receiving of the tribute
Whether literal or symbolic, the crown will be based upon revelation of the truth and the recognition of the task. When Jesus himself looks at us and says, 'Well done,' I want to hear that.

The pursuit of the reward
Paul takes this reward very seriously. He looks for any opportunity to pursue it. Back in verses 17 and 18 he shows his keenness. He says, 'If I preach voluntarily (which in this case he did not because he had to do it), I have a reward.' Then in verse 22, he says, 'To the weak I became weak, to win the weak. I have become all things to all men so that by all possible means I might save some'. It is not for nothing, he says. He

does not run aimlessly. That is like a person with no fixed goal, or a person running who loses sight of the finish line. He likens it also to someone in the boxing ring. One does not shadow-box: he is looking for the telling blow. And so Paul says we are in a fight - 'I do not fight like a man beating the air'.

There can be no doubt that Paul was in pursuit of the prize. What a day it will be when we see Paul receive his prize. I want to see that: I would like to be as close as possible when Paul gets his prize. When he wrote verse 27 he was not so sure about his chances, but when he wrote to Timothy at the end of his life, he says, 'I've fought a good fight; I've kept the faith. There is laid up for me a crown of righteousness'.

A worthy prize

It is a prize worth looking for; it is a prize worth fighting for; it is a prize worth waiting for. Some may feel that it is too late for you and that too many years have been wasted. But Paul does not write these words in 1 Corinthians to mock. He allows us to redeem the time so even when this new lifestyle with its new objective is difficult, we can be assured of the prize. And that is to hear Jesus say, 'Well done' - a prize well worth waiting for.

19

Success Under A Cloud

No, I beat my body and make it my slave so that after I have preached to others, I myself will not be disqualified for the prize. For I do not want you to be ignorant of the fact, brothers, that our forefathers were all under the cloud and they all passed through the sea. They were all baptized into Moses in the cloud and in the sea. They all ate the same spiritual food and drank the same spiritual drink; for they drank from the spiritual rock that accompanied them, and that rock was Christ. Nevertheless, God was not pleased with most of them; their bodies were scattered over the desert (1 Corinthians 9:27-10:5).

In our final chapter we look at Paul's chief Old Testament illustration of how people can be saved and lose their reward. Having stated how he himself fears the loss of the prize he turns to an ancient generation that depicts not only the possibility of history being repeated but what actually happened. It's Paul's exhibit A: Israel in the wilderness.

In the first verse of 1 Corinthian 10, there is a little Greek word, *gar*. It speaks louder in the Greek than it does in English for it means 'go back' and here it connects the two chapters together. Remember in the original Greek there were no chapters or verses, they did not have commas or full stops. So we can read the first part of this chapter's study as one sentence without any break: 'No, I beat my body and make it my slave so that after I preach to others, I myself will not be disqualified for the prize *for* I do not want you to be ignorant of the fact, brothers, that our forefathers were all under the cloud, and that they all passed through the sea'.

In the latter part of verse 27, Paul uses the word, *hupopiazo*, which literally means 'to strike under the eye'. And we all know what happens when a person is struck under the eye - he gets a black eye. For that reason there have been those who have translated 1 Corinthians 9:27, 'I beat my body black and blue', for he uses it, he says, to refer to his body.

Subjugation of the body

Paul intends to subdue his competitor, his opponent. Now who might his opponents be? We are all in a race - are we trying to outdo one another? No. Not at all. In this race every single one of us can receive that crown, that reward, that prize. So our competition, Paul says, is our bodies. He says, 'I beat it and make it my slave'. The word, 'slave', is the translation of the Greek word, *doulos*. And so he regards his body as a bad master if it is not made to be a good servant. It must be made the slave of the spirit.

Paul is not meaning here that we get to heaven because we beat our bodies black and blue, but according to Paul we could miss the prize if we do not. And the prize was very important to him. You may say, 'Well, I just don't want the prize that much!' I can only reply, Paul did.

Behind Paul's thinking are three principles. First, Paul knew that being an apostle, being a preacher, did not *guarantee* him the prize. In fact, according to James it makes it worse, as we discovered earlier. So the higher profile you have, the greater gift, the more you are called to do, the harder it is to get the prize.

Paul knew also that God is *no respecter of persons*, and therefore will not bend the rule for anybody. Now if there were ever a soul that ever lived that you would think God would bend the rule for, it would be this man, the apostle Paul. Look at the way he suffers. He says back in chapter 4:11-12, 'To this hour we go hungry and thirsty, we are in rags, we are brutally treated, we are homeless. We work hard with our hands ...' Surely that ought to move the heart of God to say, 'Well, Paul, because you have worked so hard, when it comes to the prize I'm not going to be so strict with you'. But it is the opposite. In fact it is the way it is described in Luke 17:10: So you also when you have done everything you were told to do should say, "We are unworthy servants; we have only done our duty."

As we have noted, Paul's greatest competitor was not his fellow-Christians but his very own body. He is aware of the danger for he says with some violence, 'I beat my body, make it my slave, so that after I have preached to others, I myself will not be disqualified for the prize'. In other words, it is possible to be a success as a preacher but that success could be under a cloud, not because the preaching lacked eloquence, or truth, or converts, but because of a *failure in personal holiness*.

Do you ever ask why preachers fall into sin? It is happening all the time. They become presumptuous and let success go to their heads. They let the devil in and they forget God who put them there. It happens because they ignore this verse. For you can preach to others, see them converted; you can see them grow in grace. But Paul says it does not mean that the prize is automatic. The convert might get it but the preacher might not.

Some preachers who ignore this verse seem to think of themselves as being the exception and above the rule. They think they are above the word, above the law, above the principle, and they say, 'Well, it couldn't happen to me!' Or sometimes they think that God will not let it happen to them. Yet Paul was sobered by the real possibility of failure, not in terms of numbers - he preached to thousands; not in terms of founding churches - he founded half a dozen or more churches in the Mediterranean area; not in terms of his gift - it was working and he could write letters all over the Mediterranean world, which would become two-thirds of the New Testament, and his doctrine was sound. And yet he was sobered by the awesome possibility of being a spiritual and moral failure that would put his otherwise success under a cloud.

Paul could have referred to any number of Old Testament examples of this principle; we all know them, they illustrate the same thing. But Paul chose the example of 600,000 Israelites. These were the same people who kept the Passover, who crossed over the Red Sea on dry land. But in the wilderness, in the desert, they rose up against God, whereby God said, 'I swear in my wrath they will not enter into my rest'. The rest referred to in Hebrews 3 and 4 is an analogy of the same principle.

These people, the children of Israel, had known success of a different sort, as we will see, and their success was also under a cloud. In this case, the cloud was God's own anointing: 'For I do not want you to be ignorant of the fact, brothers, that our forefathers were all under the cloud, and that they all passed through the sea'.

They had tasted of the good word of God and the powers of the world to come. They were made partakers of the Holy Spirit, but they had fallen, says Paul, in 1 Corinthians 10:5: 'God was not pleased with most of them. Their bodies were scattered over the desert'. And when he says, most of them, you can call that another British understatement: it turns out that it was 599,998 he was not pleased with, only two went into the Promised Land: Joshua and Caleb.

And so they became Paul's illustration of how one can lose the prize. It won't do to switch analogies and say that in verse 27 Paul is referring to the prize but in chapter 10 he is referring to losing salvation. No, it is consistent, it is all coherent, it is all straightforward. Paul is showing that he himself was a converted man but could lose the prize. And what he feared for himself was in fact what happened to the Israelites.

So what was their success? Well, the greatest success that is recorded in the Old Testament is victory over Pharaoh and deliverance from bondage. By faith, they defeated Pharaoh, kept the Passover and crossed the Red Sea on dry land, after which Pharaoh's army drowned.

Incidentally, Paul says '*our* forefathers'. It is very interesting to me that he is saying to these Greeks, 'your ancestors are the children of Israel'. For believers are the true Israel of God. Never forget that you are a Jew. We are the true Israel and our ancestry goes right back to there.

I think all Americans are interested in their family trees. They come over here to find their roots - forgive us but we are bit like that, I did it too. I go back to John Kendall of 1637, an Englishman; my maternal grandfather though, was Irish, and so I am a little of both. You may be interested in your ancestry but Paul says to these Greeks, 'Here is yours'. And once you become a Christian, your family tree begins to matter so this is why you want to learn about your history. So know your Old Testament.

Deliverance from bondage
So we come now to the main part of the chapter. Deliverance from bondage is the best way to describe what had happened to the children of Israel. It is a description of what went on in that era when they crossed the Red Sea on dry land.

Their redemption is what is relevant for us. It is so easy for some to say, 'Well I don't need to worry about this because I'm not an apostle, I'm not a preacher', but Paul is referring to ordinary people who followed Moses and were baptised into Moses, which means authenticating his leadership. But they had come a long way as some of you have. How far had they come?

God calls them 'his redeemed people'. They were 'bought back', in fact. In Exodus 6:6, he says, 'I am the LORD, and I will bring you out from under the yoke of the Egyptians. I will free you from being slaves to them, and I will redeem you with an outstretched arm ...'

The first thing then we can say about their redemption, is that it was *undeserved*. The same people that God promises to redeem had just been complaining to Moses: 'May the LORD look upon you and judge you'. They said to Moses, 'You have made us a stench to Pharaoh and his officials, and have put a sword in their hand to kill us' (Exodus 5:21). And yet look what God did for them.

It was also an *underwritten* redemption because in chapter 12:13 we find these famous words: 'The blood will be a sign for you on the houses where you are; and when I see the blood, I will pass over you. No destructive plague will touch you when I strike Egypt.' It was underwritten by blood.

Their redemption was also *undertaken*. This is something often forgotten. In Exodus 12:28 we read that the Israelites did just what the LORD commanded Moses and Aaron. There could have been a revolt; there could have been those who said, 'I just don't know about this idea of blood being sprinkled'. There could have been murmuring amongst them. But there was not. They did not revolt.

It was also a *universal* redemption because several times in these verses, from 1 to 5, the Greek word, *pontes*, is used, 'all'. He is wanting all of us to know that every single one of them were under the blood, not a single one excluded.

Their renewal

Paul also wants to speak of the Israelites' renewal. God did this by means of his cloud. It is interesting that in Psalm 105:39 we read that God spread out a cloud as a covering. So Paul could say that they were all under the cloud.

This shows a *supernatural* renewal. In Exodus 13:21-22, we read these words: 'By day the LORD went ahead of them in a pillar of cloud to guide them on their way and by night in a pillar of fire to give them light, so that they could travel by day or night. Neither the pillar of cloud by day nor the pillar of fire by night left its place in front of the people'.

It was also a *stabilising* renewal. In chapter 14:19 we read, 'Then the angel of God, who had been travelling in front of Israel's army, withdrew and went behind them. The pillar of cloud also moved from in front and stood behind them, coming between the armies of Egypt and Israel. Throughout the night the cloud brought darkness to the one side and light to the other side; so that neither went near the other all night long.' They were protected and shielded by the cloud.

The passage in Exodus 14:21-22 is a very dramatic one and describes the *spectacular* nature of the Israelites' escape. 'Then Moses stretched out his hand over the sea, and all that night the LORD drove the sea back with a strong east wind and turned it into dry land. The waters were divided, and the Israelites went through the sea on dry ground, with a wall of water on their right and on their left.'

And yet there is more. It was a *specific* renewal, for Paul writes in verse 2, 'They were all baptised into Moses'. What does that mean: 'They were all baptised into Moses, in the cloud and in the sea'? Well, Moses is seen here as a type of Christ. This parallel is drawn in John 1:17: 'For the law was given through Moses; grace and truth came through Jesus Christ'. There is also the analogy in Hebrews 3:1-6 of Moses and Christ. Moses was faithful; Christ was faithful, but Christ is worthy of more glory than Moses.

But what was required of the children of Israel? They had to give allegiance to Moses, as we do to Christ. And Paul says they were baptised into Moses, so that we read in Exodus 14:31, 'And when the Israelites saw the great power of the LORD displayed against the Egyptians, the people feared the LORD and put their trust in him and in Moses his servant'. And when Paul says they were baptised into Moses, the Greek shows that their being baptised was voluntary. It shows a willingness to give themselves in baptism into Moses.

Paul then is describing converted people; something had happened to those who honoured the blood. In fact, in Hebrews 11:29, we read, 'By faith the people passed through the Red Sea as on dry land; but when the Egyptians tried to do so, they were drowned'. Hebrews 11, the 'faith' chapter, says that the people who went across did it by faith. Not only that, they had beheld God's power at the Red Sea and they honoured Moses. What a beginning!

So this then was their deliverance from bondage. Yet great as this was, it did not keep the children of Israel from coming short of the prize. And this can be true of us too. Some of us have known an intimacy with God; some of us have known a closeness to him; some of us have seen remarkable answers to prayer; some of us have seen miracles in our lives, and we know God alone did that.

But what has happened since? Have you just taken for granted that because God was with you, he is still with you? Have you just assumed because you had such a beginning, that it does not matter whether you continue to listen to his voice? Remember, you are no different from all the people under the cloud.

Demonstration of blessing

Some of you have known great blessing of God and that brings me to the second point: not only the deliverance from bondage, but God's demonstration of blessing. Paul could say, 'When I came to you, I came with weakness and trembling, but God came in a demonstration of power', and those Corinthians had seen God at work mightily.

What kind of blessing was this then? Paul says, in verse 2, 'They were all baptised into Moses, in the cloud'. Now I think there is a danger of overloading the symbolic - we can push something too far - but it is arguable that this could be the Old Testament equivalent and a way of describing what we today would call baptism in the Spirit, because he says they were baptised in the cloud. For the cloud was the *anointing*. Hebrews 6:4 talks about those who were partakers of the Holy Spirit, a description of consumable spiritual progress.

We are not talking about babes in Christ, so what do you suppose is Paul's point? It is that not only can you be a preacher and lose the prize, you can enjoy great spiritual progress and lose the prize. I have been convinced for years that Hebrews 6 is not only describing true Christians, but mature Christians.[1] Far from the counterfeit, he is talking about those who had come to know God more than most. It is so scary.

So they had undergone baptism in the cloud but that was no guarantee of the prize. On top of all that had happened to them - keeping the Passover, passing through the Red Sea by faith - it did not keep them from coming short of the prize.

Their blessing included being *assured* that they were the people of God. Again and again God calls them 'my people'.

They were preserved also by God. In fact, we read that:

---

1. Dr. Kendall will examine this important section of Hebrews in his next book for Christian Focus, to be published in 1994.

'They all ate the same spiritual food and drank the same
spiritual drink' which is a reference to the manna of Exodus 16.
It was manna which enabled them to survive in the desert. How
are 600,000 people going to live in a wilderness? God gave
them manna. And he gave them water (Exodus 17). He
provided their other basic need by a miracle and gave water
from a rock. God preserved them and they were assured of his
provision for them.

I think one of the most interesting verses is Joshua 5:12 and
some day I am going to preach on it. It says the manna stopped
the day after they entered Canaan, after they ate the food from
the land. Once God's provision was no longer required in these
ways, it stopped. This was further assurance for them that God
was caring and looking after them.

The blessing was also *affirmation*, for Paul says that the
rock that followed them was *Christ*. This is affirmation,
beyond which no greater could be conceived. This is a clear
reference to the pre-existence of Christ. The *logos*, the eternal
Word, before he was made flesh, manifested himself and
displayed his glory in the desert!

And so these same people were not only baptised into
Moses and baptised in the cloud, but they also partook of
Christ. This is Christ in the Old Testament. And so Paul thus
shows Israel in the desert as exhibit A, of what it is like to be
saved. And yet they have their success under a cloud; they fail
to win the prize.

Disapproval of their behaviour

In verse 5, finally, Paul speaks of God's disapproval for most of
the children of Israel: 'nevertheless God was not pleased with
most of them. Their bodies were scattered over the desert'.

The body

Why do you think Paul says, 'I beat my body and make it my slave', and now he says their *bodies* were scattered over the desert? I can give you four reasons.

First, the body is a *spiritual temple*: 'Do you not know that your body is a temple of the Holy Spirit, who is in you, whom you have received from God' (1 Corinthians 6:19).

Second, the body is the *servant of trust*. Paul said, 'I make the body my slave'. I find it interesting in 1 Corinthians 9:25 that Paul refers to strict training and in verse 27 to the body being tamed - he says 'I beat my body and make it my slave'. So our bodies are given to us as a trust from God.

Yet it is also the *stuff of temptation*. It is called the 'instrument of sin' in Romans 6:13.

Finally, the body is the *source of the tongue*, and so much that happened in the wilderness was because they murmured. James 3:6 says: 'The tongue also is a fire, a world of evil among the parts of the *body*'.

In Psalm 95:11 God said, 'I swear in my wrath, they will not enter my rest'. Likewise these Corinthians were in danger of missing out on the prize. The question is: are we? What grips me, and I pray it will grip you, is that Paul believed in God's ruthless impartiality. Let that grip you. At the judgment seat of Christ Paul knew that his own present intimacy with God did not mean that he could tell God what to do. Paul's intimacy with God did not result in an over-familiarity with him, whereby he says, 'Well, it can't happen to me'. Paul did not have indemnity because he was an apostle; preachers do not have indemnity because they seek conversions; high profile Christians have no indemnity; your years of Christian service are not going to guarantee that you get the prize.

Luther said, 'When I get to heaven, I expect to be surprised three times. There will be those in heaven I thought wouldn't be there, and there will be some missing I thought would be there, but the greatest surprise will be that I am there myself'. But could I paraphrase that one more time? I suspect there will be three surprises: some will receive the prize I thought would not, some will not be rewarded that I thought would, but the greatest surprise will be if I receive it.

And I pray that we all do.

(P) 19/2/04.   28/7/04 15/12/04 11/4/05 20/10/05
25/5/04   31/8/04 14/1/05   9/5/05 9/11/05
24/6/04   1/10/04 11/2/05 12/6/05
            9/11/04 12/3/05 15/7/05